KATHY SMITH'S
MOVING THROUGH MENOPAUSE

KATHY SMITH'S MOVING THROUGH MENOPAUSE

The Complete Program for Exercise, Nutrition, and Total Wellness

Kathy Smith

with Robert Miller

WARNER BOOKS

An AOL Time Warner Company

PUBLISHER'S NOTE: Neither this exercise program nor any other exercise program should be followed without first consulting a health care professional. If you have any special conditions requiring attention, you should consult with your health care professional regularly regarding possible modification of the program contained in this book.

Warner Books, Inc., 1271 Avenue of the Americas, New York, NY 10020

 An AOL Time Warner Company

Printed in the United States of America

ISBN 0-7394-2510-2

Book design and text composition by H. Roberts Design
Cover design by Brigid Pearson
Interior photos by Cory Sorenson

Acknowledgments

Unlike any other project, this book has taken the time, energy, and effort of so many people to help me get my arms around the subject and to produce a book that I believe represents a balanced look at such a complicated topic.

Rob Miller and I have collaborated before and will hopefully do so again. He organizes disparate, complicated, and seemingly unrelated information, and makes it gel. He's a talented and dedicated writer, and a gem of a person.

This project could not have happened without Trisha Peck. She provided invaluable research and editorial assistance from start to finish, not only on this book, but also on my menopause video.

I'd like to also acknowledge several people for their help and expertise in preparing the material for this book: Paula Bernstein, M.D., Ann Christie, Ph.D., Daniel Cosgrove, M.D., Betty Dodson, Ph.D., Prudence Hall, M.D., Mary Hardy, M.D., Dr. Kenneth R. Pelletier, and Beth Rothenberg.

To Trina Lewis for keeping everybody in the loop and on deadline, to Suzie Dimpfl for her love of movement and expert eye, to Mark Stephens for his understanding of yoga and its effects on the body, to Diana Baroni for her belief in this project, and finally to Kate and Perrie for the laughter and meaning you bring to my life—thank you.

Contents

Chapter 1
A Change for the Better

Every twenty-nine days for the past thirty years, my body has faithfully prepared itself to become pregnant. Two of those occasions resulted in the births of my daughters. The other four-hundred-plus times have provided a kind of vital pulse throughout my adult life. A steady internal rhythm, dependable as the seasons.

This cycle is something you live with so long it becomes an inseparable part of you. You know just how much you'll bleed, how much you'll bloat; you know which day of the month you'll burst into tears for no reason, or find a pimple on your face. When that cycle finally starts to change, it's as though some natural law had been repealed. Nothing feels the same anymore—and *you* don't feel like the same person.

The strangeness of your cycle changing is just the beginning. Equally disturbing is what the changes symbolize. It's one thing to conclude, rationally, that my reproductive capacity is only part of who I am—a large and vital part, yes, but still just a part. Yet what woman can watch those first interruptions in her cycle and not feel a pang of loss? This is true at whatever age the change occurs, whether or not she has had children. That's because it marks far more than the end of reproduction.

A friend of mine, a university professor, told me: Watch a group of students over the course of a semester. The first five or six weeks drift by leisurely: The students joke around, they skip class to sunbathe. But right at week six, everything changes. Some unconscious sense tells them their time has been cut in half. Suddenly the jokes stop, the concentration level goes up, and they do the work of ten weeks in five.

My friend calls this realization the *halftime bell*. It applies not just to school, of course, but also to our lives, and there's something deep and universal about how we respond.

Sensing the Change

I began to sense this change in a kind of dream—a fitful half sleep in which I tossed and struggled, night after night, to fall back to sleep after hearing that bell toll repeatedly in my psyche.

I was having terrible bouts of insomnia. I'd always been a good sleeper, accustomed to waking up refreshed. Now, a healthy and active forty-nine-year-old woman, I felt as if a cloud hung over me. I'd toss and turn for a few hours each night and wake in the morning feeling cheated of a good night's sleep. There was a leaden heaviness in my body. I felt full of anxiety. I'd kick off the sheets; I'd pull them back up, shivering. In my journal, I charted my ordeal:

> Last night . . . disturbing sensations in my body . . . upset stomach . . . an uncomfortably warm feeling (notice I'm not using the term *hot flash;* I think I'm in denial!). Awake at 4:00, tossing until 6:30. In those hours, as I drift in and out of sleep, I have the most outrageous dreams. . . . What on earth is going on?

Deprived of sleep at night, I was a raw nerve by day. I'd see the world through layers of gauze. I'd shut the bathroom door and sob. Was I going crazy?

Relax, It's Only Menopause

Like many women, I had resisted the idea that I might be perimenopausal. *How do I know if I am? What does it mean? What will it feel like, and how long will it last?* Most of all: *What should I be doing to cope with the unique stresses of this transition?*

As someone who's spent her life promoting the benefits of a healthy lifestyle, I assumed I already knew a lot of the answers. But in many respects, this is new territory. And while it's true that the basic rules of healthy living are as important now as ever, there are new reasons for following them. Regular exercise and healthy eating now take aim at symptoms and problems I'd never encountered before. And there are *new* questions to consider—important decisions concerning various conventional or alternative medical therapies.

And so my personal exploration began and grew into this book. My goal was to design a special plan for this time in my life, one that would address all the areas on which menopause would have an impact.

In the upcoming chapters, I'll share the answers I discovered, and help you find your own answers, to help in your journey. Everyone's experience is different. Lifestyle measures are not necessarily a substitute for hormone therapy or other medication, and some women may choose to do both. However, lifestyle improvements will build a healthy foundation for *anyone* and, in that sense, they are the best medicine of all.

The goal of this book is to help you take charge of perimenopause and menopause in three ways:

- **Understand it.** Learning the facts about the physical changes you're experiencing will relieve anxiety and help you focus on how to deal with them.
- **Manage it.** Find solutions to symptoms and ways of coping with midlife issues.
- **Own it.** Accept and embrace menopause as an opportunity to make important changes in your life.

The Lifestyle Plan

When I first realized I was perimenopausal and began researching the subject, I was overwhelmed with advice and input. At every party I went to, I seemed to attract an eager group of women all bursting to share their stories. Anytime I'd drop the M word in conversation, the breathless response would be *"We gotta talk!"*

My OB/GYN immediately said, "Let me put you on a low-dose birth control." Meanwhile, the women at the parties were all asking me: "Have you tried black cohosh?" "Do you think yoga would help my sex drive?" "How much soy do you eat?" And so on, until my head started spinning.

How does anyone evaluate all this information—all the medical treatments, all the folk remedies? For me, it's been a major project. I now have an entire shelf devoted to menopause books. I've read scores of personal stories from visitors to my Web site. And for months now, I've been meeting with doctors, alternative practitioners, and other experts, interviewing them about their various philosophies.

Here's what I've learned:

I've learned that menopause is an *elusive* subject, because women's experiences differ so widely. For one friend, menopause hardly mussed her hair; for another, it was like the sky falling. One woman frightened me with vivid descriptions of having to change her sweaty sheets two and three times a night. Should I be preparing for symptoms like that?

I've also learned that, scientifically, menopause is *complex*. The physiology of hormones and their effects on the body are downright inscrutable. And as most women know, there's great controversy about whether to treat menopause with hormone replacement therapy. One camp considers HRT dangerous and unnatural; the other considers it an indispensable wonder drug.

Fortunately, in the midst of all this, everyone agrees on one thing: A healthy lifestyle is *the* most important factor of all. Good nutrition, regular exercise, a minimum of stress—these are the things that can help any woman move through menopause with relative ease.

Change Is Nothing New

For many of us, our forties is a critical, pivotal decade. It's when you either start becoming interested in health and begin doing the things that will sustain you in the long run, or (I hate to say it) you really start to go to pieces in a way that's tough to bounce back from. For women who've neglected their health, menopause comes as the coup de grâce that leaves them feeling hopeless about their bodies and about ever looking and feeling better. The natural process of aging seems to be going into a steep nosedive that they just can't pull out of.

If you're like many women, you're dreading the change. But take a closer look. You've been changing all along. In fact, there's no period of life that's not marked by physical change.

The fact is, your body naturally reaches a peak of vitality in your twenties and then begins a long and, at first, very gradual decline. Muscle mass shrinks, bone density declines—and with them strength, endurance, balance, reaction time, and mental clarity. All of these changes are developing five, ten, or even fifteen years before the hormonal fluctuations that precede menopause even *start*. They are simply the outcome of being alive. So much of what we're experiencing around menopause is really the result of these age-related changes.

This calls for some glass-half-full thinking:

I believe each of us has a *vital potential* at every stage of life—a peak level of vitality that we could be experiencing—*if* we were doing everything possible to reach it. That peak will naturally be a little lower at sixty than at thirty. That's life. But the exciting thing is this: Most of us have *so much room for improvement* that we're poised to experience huge gains in well-being, just by actualizing our potential.

By adopting healthier lifestyle habits—especially exercise and better eating—we can push our vitality higher and higher on that scale, closer to our peak potential. In this way, it is literally possible to feel better at fifty than you ever have in your life!

The point is to get you, and keep you, as close to your *full vital potential* as possible at whatever age you are.

Everyone's heard the joke about youth being wasted on the young. Middle age, though, need not be wasted on anyone: At fifty, you can have *all* the ingredients of a fulfilling life—experience, wisdom, *and* the physical vitality to do something about it.

How Much Room for Improvement Do I Have?

Just for fun, take this little test. There are no wrong answers; just be as honest as you can. This will give you an accurate picture of where you are today and how you could make healthier choices to improve your vitality.

Spot some room for improvement? The more areas you found that need improving, the more you've got to gain!

With that in mind, let's take a look at the elements of our plan. Our primary goal throughout this book is to discover how much we can improve our sense of well-being around menopause through exercise, diet, and other lifestyle modifications. Remember . . .

- If your muscles are strong . . .
- If you're lean and fit and active . . .
- If you eat good nutritious food with a wide variety of nutrients . . .
- If you keep your stress level down . . .
- If you nurture the relationships in your life and work to create good communication with the people you're close to . . .
- If you have a healthy, active sex life . . .

. . . If you do all this, you'll *still* go through menopause. But it will be a completely different experience than it otherwise would have been, and it truly can be a change for the better!

Your Vitality Profile

	DOIN' IT	WILLING TO IMPROVE	NEEDS IMPROVEMENT, BUT NOT A PRIORITY
Nonsmoker			
Moderate alcohol consumption (less than 3 drinks/day)			
Moderate coffee/caffeinated soda consumption (less than 2 cups or cans/day)			
No other substance dependencies			
Limit refined sugar to 10% of total calories			
Generally low-fat diet			
High fruit/vegetable consumption			
Eat fish at least 2x week			
Regular aerobic exercise			
Regular strength training exercise			
Good relationship with a doctor you trust			
Strong support system			
Satisfying intimate relationship			
Adequate rest and relaxation			
Satisfying hobbies, personal interests			

Vitality Prescription:

Number of areas you rated "willing to improve": _____

The Elements of the *Moving Through Menopause* Lifestyle Plan

There are three major themes of menopause: first, the immediate hormonal symptoms, such as hot flashes and mood swings; second, a need to reexamine your life and find a deeper sense of meaning; and, finally, long-term health issues, specifically heart disease and bone loss.

My *Moving Through Menopause* Plan is a simple, six-point approach that addresses all three of these themes. Let's take a look at each of the points, one by one:

• *Exercise for Physical Conditioning and Mood*

There's hardly a menopausal symptom that exercise doesn't improve: From fatigue to mental alertness, from low libido to insomnia— exercise is *my* candidate for a wonder drug. When I first got involved in running, I discovered what a miraculous mood booster it could be. I could go from "I can't do it; nobody likes me . . ." to "Hey, *I'm a superstar!*" in just forty-five minutes of running. Beyond just exercising to feel better, though, we'll cover several types of exercise aimed at other goals as well, including strength training to steel your skeleton, and Kegel exercise to keep your pelvic muscles healthy and your sex life humming.

• *Phytoestrogens and Herbs for Symptoms*

Over one quarter of today's prescription drugs are derived from plant sources, many of which were folk remedies for centuries before being "discovered" by Western medicine. Several herbs traditionally used for menopausal symptoms offer safe and effective alternatives to conventional medicine for making you more comfortable in the short term. In addition, certain foods, such as soy, contain substances that have a mild estrogenlike effect on the body, offering both short- and, possibly, even long-term health benefits.

- ## *Good Nutrition for Energy, Weight Loss, and Long-Term Health*

Healthy eating principles haven't changed. But now there's a whole new list of incentives for following them, including maintaining strong bones, easing the risk of heart disease, and countering menopausal weight gain. Good nutrition can also keep your energy high.

- ## *Attending to Your Inner Self*

More than just a physical transition, menopause is a spiritual journey. It's apt to be a time of restlessness and reassessment, when we search for positive new ways to see ourselves and our future. Coping with the psychological and emotional issues of the time is one of the major challenges of midlife.

- ## *Yoga and Relaxation Techniques*

Lowering stress is one of the best safeguards against midlife problems, and yoga provides the perfect combination of techniques to accomplish the job. In fact, yoga breathing techniques may even help with hot flashes. In one study, researchers at the Lafayette Clinic in Detroit found that paced respiration (similar to yogic breathing) reduced hot flashes by up to 40 percent. By calming the nervous system and improving circulation, yoga can pull you back from emotional plunges and rejuvenate your energy supply. In addition, certain postures affect the endocrine and reproductive systems, which can help balance erratic hormonal shifts and awaken the sex center.

- ## *HRT*

Although our focus will mainly be on improving your health through lifestyle changes, everything we'll cover can serve as a foundation for hormone replacement therapy, if you decide to go that route. I've included a chapter on HRT, so you'll have the basic information you need to discuss this very important topic with your physician.

Finally, I've provided templates of daily pages you can use to track your symptoms, your workouts, and other lifestyle improvements.

Keeping a journal is a great way to chart both physical and psychological changes.

Your Journal

A big component of my plan is your journal. Keeping a journal is a great way to review your day, making note of the people, places, and things that may have triggered hot flashes, stress, and emotional reactions. My journal has been my constant companion through perimenopause. I find that the act of writing itself releases anxiety and clears my mind of negative thinking. From time to time, I'll be giving you exercises or suggestions about issues to explore in your journal.

Your journal can take whatever form you want. It might be a bound, blank book that you fill with a thoughtful record of your experience. Or it might simply be a yellow legal pad where you can vent your feelings in frenzied scribbling, afterward crumpling the pages and throwing them away. Do whatever suits your personality or your mood. The main thing is to find a way to chart your inner journey.

Journal Exercise

WHAT WAS YOUR FIRST CLUE?

The first indication that I might be perimenopausal was a sudden shift in my sleeping patterns. It wasn't until I started exploring this issue in my journal, though, that I really got a sense of the implications and how I felt about them.

What was your *first* clue? What tipped you off that things were different in your cycle and psyche? Even if you're not certain you're perimenopausal yet, write about your intuition concerning the changes in your body.

Time to Get Moving!

However varied women's experience of menopause may be, however complex the physiologic changes, I believe it all comes down to this simple formula: The healthier you are, the easier your menopause will be. The sooner you take charge of your symptoms, the better you'll feel. And the sooner you get a running start on the long-term consequences, the better you'll feel *later,* when your symptoms are gone and life starts anew. So whether menopause is way out on the horizon, or staring you in the face, the time to start is now!

Chapter 2

Menopause:
What, When, and Why

I've never been menopausal, nor do I ever
intend to be, thank you very much.
—Fran, age sixty-five

I n talking to my friends, I realize that women my age are approaching menopause knowing very little about it—neither the science nor the experience of it. Unlike my own daughters—who will have their mom's own *book* as a reference—women of our generation, by and large, learned little or nothing about this profound life process from our mothers. It just wasn't discussed.

In this chapter, I'll try to answer most of the basic questions women ask about the cause and effects of menopause. This information will provide a good foundation for the rest of the program.

What Does It Mean?

The word *menopause* doesn't really sound like what it is. What's actually happening is not a "pause" at all, but a full stop to the reproductive cycle. It begins with a gradual shrinking of the ovaries that usually starts around age forty and speeds up in the final three to four years before menopause. Typically, this leads to a period of erratic function known as *perimenopause*, during which hormone levels may fluctuate wildly, causing a variety of symptoms. Finally, *clinical menopause* describes the moment at which egg production and menstruation cease completely.

The main feature of menopause is the decline and eventual loss of *estrogen,* one of several hormones (including *progesterone* and *testosterone*) that are manufactured in the ovaries. Working with other hormones produced in the brain, estrogen and progesterone are responsible for the monthly production and release of eggs, as well as for the buildup and shedding of the uterine lining. Estrogen and the other ovarian hormones have wide-ranging effects on tissues throughout the body. They contribute to the health of our bones, hair, skin, blood, mood, and overall sense of vitality and well-being. Although small amounts of estrogen continue to be produced in your fat tissue and adrenal glands after menopause, the sharp drop that occurs when the ovaries stop producing has both short-term and long-term effects on the body.

Reaching Menopause Naturally

As hormonal production in the ovaries slows, women may experience gaps in their menstrual cycle of up to several months. Thus, it's impossible to pinpoint the moment when menopause occurs. Your period may stop for a while, and then start up again. For clarity's sake, you're "officially" menopausal after a full year has passed since your last period. *Menopausal* means you're now in the phase of life after menopause.

Surgical or Induced Menopause

Menopause can also be induced or occur as the result of certain surgical procedures. Surgical menopause results when a woman has a hysterectomy that includes removal of both ovaries, a procedure called a bilateral oophorectomy. This is a common treatment for fibroid tumors and other disorders; each year, according to the North American Menopause Association, close to half a million women reach menopause this way. The symptoms following surgical removal of the ovaries are often more intense than those of natural menopause, because of the sudden and drastic loss of estrogen.

Menopause can also be triggered by medical procedures or drugs, including pelvic radiation therapy and chemotherapy; in about 30 percent of women who experience this, the effect is temporary. Short-term, reversible menopause can also be induced by excessive exercise, dieting, and by taking hormones that suppress ovarian function.

When Does It Normally Occur?

Natural menopause—not induced by surgery or other outside factors—usually occurs anywhere from your early forties to late fifties. The average age in the Western world is 51.4 years; by that time, about 50 percent of women have reached it. By age fifty-five, nearly 90 percent of women are menopausal. Less commonly, a woman may reach menopause naturally in her thirties, or as late as her sixties. Menopause before age forty is considered premature or early menopause, and is usually caused by factors such as surgical removal of the ovaries, radiation therapy, smoking, and certain diseases. Interestingly, the average age of menopause hasn't changed over the past few centuries, despite increased life expectancy.

Perimenopause

Perimenopause is the period of time people usually mean when they say someone is "going through menopause." In fact, it's the transitional phase *leading* to menopause. The average age for starting perimenopause is 47.5 years. If you're reaching this age now, you're part of the largest wave in history to do so. According to U.S. Census data, as of July 2000 there were twenty million women in the forty-five to fifty-five age range, who would most likely be at or closely approaching menopause.

ASK YOUR DOCTOR

For women who have their ovaries removed before forty, the premature loss of estrogen's protective effects against heart disease and osteoporosis may increase the risk of those diseases. Hormone therapy may help minimize the symptoms and health risks associated with surgical menopause (more about this in chapter 12).

DEFINITIONS

Perimenopause: A period of several years leading up to menopause during which you're still menstruating, but are having fluctuations in estrogen levels that may produce hot flashes or other symptoms. Average age is about forty-seven.

Menopause: Technically, the cessation of menses and the end of reproductive activity. For practical purposes, it's the phase of life beginning one year after your last period. *Reaching menopause* means reaching that one-year point. *In menopause* or *menopausal* both mean being past the one-year point.

Premenopausal: Refers to any time before reproductivity ends.

Postmenopausal: Refers to the phase of life following menopause.

How Can I Tell if I'm in Perimenopause?

In the last chapter, I described how a bout of insomnia after a lifetime of sound sleep made me begin to suspect that I might be perimenopausal. For most women, physical symptoms such as irregular periods and hot flashes, as well as vaginal dryness, mood changes, and memory loss, are clues that their estrogen and other hormones are fluctuating. If you're in your late forties, are still menstruating, and are beginning to experience some of the symptoms characteristic of erratic hormone levels (I'll describe these in a moment), you may be in perimenopause.

Sometimes perimenopausal symptoms are difficult to distinguish from those of PMS or depression. To help determine your status, your doctor may recommend a blood test to check your level of follicle-stimulating hormone, or FSH.

The FSH Test

FSH is the "messenger" hormone the brain sends to spur your ovaries into producing more estrogen. When estrogen levels are down, FSH levels go up. A high FSH level, therefore, could be a signal of menopause.

Before menopause, FSH levels rarely rise above 10 MIU/ml. If your doctor finds your level is over 15 MIU/ml, he or she will probably suspect you to be in perimenopause. If it's as high as 30 to 40 MIU/ml, your doctor will most likely inform you that you've reached menopause.

Your FSH level is not always a reliable indicator, however, because fluctuating estrogen levels during perimenopause can frequently be *higher* than normal, as well as lower. Still, when considered with your symptoms and medical history, an FSH reading can help your doctor piece together a picture of where you stand.

Women taking oral contraceptives will need to switch temporarily to a nonhormonal form of birth control in order to obtain accurate FSH test results.

Short-Term Symptoms

Let's start with the good news: At least 10 percent of women reach menopause abruptly and without obvious symptoms. And many more have a reasonably easy time: Several surveys report that as many as 15 to 25 percent of women reach menopause without any menopause-related complaints.

And then, of course, there's the rest of us. Menopause is highly variable, and everyone's experience of it is likely to be unique. Some of the symptoms often associated with this transition are listed below. Those toward the top of the list are more common.

- Skipped periods
- Heavier or lighter periods
- Increased PMS
- Hot flashes (also called flushes)
- Vaginal dryness
- Mood swings
- Night sweats
- Restless sleep
- Lack of concentration
- Loss of libido
- Irritability
- Muscle aches and pains
- Infections of the genitourinary system
- Crawling skin
- Fatigue
- Headaches
- Memory loss
- Heart palpitations

Long-Term Risks

The loss of reproductive levels of estrogen can have profound long-term effects on the

---

FACTORS AFFECTING MENOPAUSE

The timing of menopause is determined by:

- Genetics—Family history is a good indicator: You're likely to reach menopause at about the same age as your mother.
- Tobacco—Smoking causes the ovaries to shut down about one to two years early, in some cases more. The longer and heavier you smoke, the greater the effect.

Menopause *may* be accelerated by:

- Never having been pregnant
- Having a short menstrual cycle
- Prescription antidepressants
- Toxic chemical exposure
- Treatment of childhood cancer with pelvic radiation

Menopause *may* be delayed by:

- Having a high percentage of body fat

Menopause is *not* affected by:

- The age at which you had your first period
- Contraceptives
- Socioeconomic status, marital status, or race

body, because it removes a layer of protection against certain diseases. This can be happening even if you're not experiencing any overt symptoms.

Heart Disease

Researchers believe the body's estrogen protects the heart by improving the balance of blood lipids in favor of HDLs (the "good cholesterol"). Estrogen also dilates the coronary arteries, improving blood flow to the heart. The sharp drop in estrogen at menopause can pose a threat for those already at risk for coronary heart disease. While hormone replacement therapy can reduce heart disease risk up to 50 percent, exercise, proper diet, and other lifestyle steps can help, too.

Bone Loss

Bone loss comes with age. A woman's natural estrogen exerts a protective effect on her bones, however, by helping slow the rate at which calcium is broken down. As estrogen levels decline, the rate of bone loss increases, and may reach as high as 3 to 4 percent per year around the time of menopause. An alarming 40 percent of women over fifty suffer bone fractures—often with disastrous consequences to their quality of life. Several good options exist for women at risk for bone loss, which we'll explore in more detail in chapter 7.

Incontinence

Stress incontinence, or the leakage of urine when laughing, coughing, or sneezing, is a common problem in the years following menopause. Loss of estrogen leads to a decline in muscle tone and tissue strength in and around the urethra, making it difficult to restrict the flow of urine. This can be treated with surgery, but at least 50 percent of women can also treat the problem successfully using only exercise and over-the-counter products. I'll describe these in conjunction with other changes to the vagina in chapter 6.

Cognitive Function

Some researchers believe there is a link between loss of estrogen and a decline in long-term cognitive health, and speculate that estrogen replacement may help prevent or delay the development of Alzheimer's disease. According to the National Institute on Aging, animal and observational studies of estrogen's benefits in this area have been promising but not conclusive, and more research needs to be done. Meanwhile, brain-healthy lifestyle habits include staying active—both physically and mentally—and taking antioxidant supplements (especially vitamin E).

It's Not a Disease—But Take Charge, Anyway

The idea that menopause is somehow a "disease" or malfunction has deep roots in our society. Fortunately, this attitude is changing.

Physically, menopause is a normal biological event—a particularly dramatic blip on the timeline of a woman's natural aging. It seems crazy to brand something a *disease* when the healthiest woman alive couldn't avoid it. No amount of spinach or step aerobics can extend the life of your ovaries. Like it or not, this is something nature intends.

Yet as my friend Paige told me, during her fifth hot flash that day, "I know it's not a disease, but sometimes it sure *feels* like one." And that's the point: However normal it may be, the symptoms are very real. That's why I like to balance these two points of view:

• Menopause is *not* a disease. Nothing has gone "wrong" with our bodies.

At the same time . . .

• We should do everything we can to reduce the symptoms and long-term health risks associated with menopause, to ensure the highest quality of life. For some women, this may mean hormone replacement therapy. In addition, though, there's a whole arsenal of lifestyle changes and alternative remedies that I feel *everyone* should take advantage of.

Menopause is not a disease, but it *is* a call to action. The forecast is bright. According to a 1998 poll taken by the North American Menopause Society, *post*menopausal women reported that they felt happier and more fulfilled than ever before. This may be due to a variety of factors:

- Greater sense of freedom and choice
- The chance to focus on personal goals beyond simply being a mom
- No more menstrual periods or PMS
- A sex life free of contraception and the fear of pregnancy

Menopause is a natural event, and it *can* be a highly positive one, brimming with possibilities—so let's get started. The best way to get through it is to get *on* it!

Chapter 3

Vital Statistics:
Your Self-Assessment
Project

Many perimenopausal women report feeling vaguely "out of sync" with themselves and the world around them, but find it hard to figure out exactly what's going on. They simply know they're feeling confused, anxious—possibly even depressed.

Taking a good, objective look at yourself and your situation is the first step toward getting things under control again. That's what the questionnaires in this chapter are designed to do. They will:

- Help you assess your symptoms.
- Help you spot risk factors for serious disease.
- Lead you through a process of self-reflection designed to reveal points about your general health, your lifestyle, and your attitudes about menopause and midlife.

Besides raising your own awareness, these questionnaires may help you identify important questions to ask your doctor. The more your doctor understands about your circumstances, the more helpful he or she can be.

Look at these assessments as the first step toward giving yourself the quality of life you deserve.

Symptoms

On the following chart, rate any symptoms you're now having according to severity and frequency.

Severity Values

0=none

1=mild (Other women seem to have it worse.)

2=moderate (I seem to be going through what everyone else is.)

3=severe (Other women should look at me and count their blessings.)

Severity means the extent of the symptom. For example, for "night sweats," a rating of 1 might mean *damp*, 2 might mean *wet*, and 3 *drenched*.

In addition to severity and frequency, the key issue here is what I call the *bother factor*. A symptom can be mild and yet still bothersome if it's affecting important areas of your life. On the other hand, something that has disturbed you tremendously may trouble you less after you realize that it's perfectly normal and won't last forever. Making this distinction will help you decide where to target your efforts at relief.

What Your Answers Mean

If your symptoms aren't totally driving you nuts, you may be able to bring them under control using just lifestyle changes such as exercise, diet, and various alternative remedies. On the other hand, if they're seriously taking the joy out of life, your answers will help you and your doctor decide what steps to take to start improving your quality of life. You may be a good candidate for hormone replacement therapy, which can be used in conjunction with the program in this book. You may want to repeat this exercise a few months from now, after beginning the program, to see what's changed and how your efforts at relief are going.

Disease Risk Profiles

Because the drop in estrogen levels at menopause increases your risk for osteoporosis and heart disease, it's good to identify any other risk factors you

SYMPTOM	SEVERITY (0–3)	FREQUENCY (X PER WEEK)	BOTHER FACTOR (Y/N)
Hot flashes/night sweats			
Irregular bleeding			
Vaginal dryness			
Urinary problems			
Sleeplessness			
Anxiety			
Irritability/anger			
Depression			
Fatigue			
PMS			
Headaches			
Pain in muscles or joints			
Concentration problems			
Crawling skin			
Other:			

might have for these diseases. The charts on the following pages will help you do that, so you can decide how to target your efforts at reducing risk.

About Your Risk Profiles

Discovering you have risk factors for these diseases might feel a little scary at first. Still, it's better to know about them, because your awareness will allow you to take steps to prevent future problems. Both heart disease and bone loss risk can be helped considerably by exercise, healthy eating, and other lifestyle changes. In addition, your doctor may urge you to consider hormone replacement therapy (HRT) or other medication as a precaution. This is an individual decision and should be made only after careful consideration; I'll discuss some of the issues involved in chapter 12. For more on long-term health risks, see chapter 7.

Osteoporosis

RISK FACTOR	YES	NO	DON'T KNOW
Small, thin, frame			
Caucasian or Asian			
Family members with osteoporosis			
Early menopause (before age 40)			
Surgical menopause			
More than 6 months of no periods during reproductive years (not counting pregnancies)			
Never having been pregnant			
Postmenopausal			
Long-Term Medication Use:			
Corticosteroids (such as prednisone or cortisone)			
Anticonvulsants			
Antacids containing aluminum			
Larger than usual doses of thyroid medication			
Diseases:			
Hyperthyroidism			
Cushing's disease			
Acromegaly			
Hypogonadism			
Hyperparathyroidism			
Insulin-dependent diabetes			

Osteoporosis (continued)

RISK FACTOR	YES	NO	DON'T KNOW
Lifestyle Risks			
Physically inactive (less than 1 hr. strenuous exercise/week)			
Smoking			
High-protein diet (more than 25% of calorie intake)			
High consumption of phosphorus-containing sodas			
Alcohol use (more than 2 drinks/day)			
Low dietary calcium intake			
Lack of sufficient vitamin D			

Number of factors I answered yes to: _____

Not all these factors carry equal risk. However, if you answered yes to three or more of them, you are most likely at moderate risk for bone loss or osteoporosis. I recommend you discuss any yes answers with your doctor.

Number of factors I answered yes to that I could change: _____ (Circle them and enter the total here.)

Heart Disease

RISK FACTOR	YES	NO	DON'T KNOW
Family history of heart attack, stroke, or coronary bypass before age 65			
African American descent			
Diabetes			
Surgical removal of ovaries			
Postmenopausal			
Elevated homocysteine level			
Blood clots easily			
Tendency to accumulate fat in the upper body (apple shape)			
Lifestyle Risks			
Smoking			
High blood pressure			
Alcohol use (more than 2 drinks/day)			
Obesity (more than 30% over ideal weight)			
High cholesterol level (more than 200)			
High triglyceride level (more than 250)			
Physically inactive			
High stress level			
High-fat diet			

Number of factors I answered yes to: _____

Not all these factors carry equal risk. However, if you answered yes to three or more of them, you may be at moderate risk for heart disease. Again, I recommend discussing any yes answers with your doctor.

Number of factors I answered yes to that I could change: _____ (Circle them and enter the total here.)

General Health

In many ways, the state of your health before menopause will determine how you experience the transition. Your answers to the following questions can help provide some perspective on the severity or extent of the changes that may occur.

Menstrual

❏ Yes ❏ No   I typically experience significant PMS.

❏ Yes ❏ No   I frequently experience irregular periods.

Diseases or Other Conditions

List any diseases or physical conditions that currently affect your energy, mood, or general well-being:

_____

_____

Sleep

For most of my life I've been a:

❏ Sound sleeper

❏ Restless sleeper

❏ Light sleeper

Over the course of a week, I tend to average _____ hours of sleep a night.

I believe I need _____ hours of sleep to feel my best.

Energy

Your energy level could best be described:

❏ People say I'm a bundle of energy.

❏ Most days I have the energy to do what I need to do.

❏ Seems like half the time I'm just dragging my butt around.

ASK YOUR DOCTOR

In this book, we're focused mainly on lifestyle measures. But when you're weighing the question of whether HRT is right for you, you'll also want to discuss with your doctor your risk for other diseases, including cancer, diabetes, and Alzheimer's disease.

Emotions/Personality

❐ Yes ❐ No   I've always been a generally happy, emotionally well-balanced person.

❐ Yes ❐ No   I've always had regular bouts of the blues.

❐ Yes ❐ No   I've always been highly strung.

❐ Yes ❐ No   I spend too much time worrying about the future, or things I can't change.

❐ Yes ❐ No   Most of the time I welcome change.

❐ Yes ❐ No   Most of the time I prefer the stability of things staying as they are.

I would say I tend to display the following traits: (check any that apply)

❐ Competitiveness

❐ Aggressiveness

❐ Sense of urgency

❐ Perfectionism

❐ Tendency to respond angrily when criticized or treated unfairly

Note: There is evidence that Type-A personality traits such as these are associated with higher LDL levels and therefore may raise the risk of coronary artery disease.

❐ Yes ❐ No   I'm currently seeing a psychotherapist or counselor.

❐ Yes ❐ No   I probably should be in therapy/counseling.

How might therapy/counseling help you right now?

_____

Weight

My weight is approximately _____.

I believe my ideal weight would be _____.

Sex

How would you rate your sex life?

❐ I enjoy my sex life.

❐ My sex life could be improved.

❐ What sex life?

Frequency of sexual activity (including masturbation) _____x/week

The word that best describes my sex life is: _____.

About Your General Health Profile

Menopause can often amplify existing conditions. For instance, PMS can become more pronounced; if you've never had it, you're likely to have an easier time than someone who's been experiencing it all along. Emotions, too, can be exaggerated; if you've always been prone to extreme highs and lows, you may be in for more of a roller coaster than someone who's naturally even-keeled. Likewise, if excess weight has been an issue in the past, it may become more of an issue now. On the plus side, women with active, satisfying sex lives tend to have an easier time maintaining them. Of course, all these factors (and others) interrelate, so they can't be taken as predictors, only tendencies. Again, view your responses in a spirit of self-awareness.

Midlife Stress

Besides the strain of hormonal changes, what other stress are you dealing with?

❏ Yes   Have you recently changed, or are you planning to change, jobs or careers?

❏ Yes   Have you recently changed residence?

❏ Yes   Are you caring for young or adolescent children?

❏ Yes   Do you have adult children who've recently moved out, or back home?

❏ Yes   Are you responsible for taking care of parents or grandparents?

❏ Yes   Have you recently experienced a death of someone close to you?

❏ Yes   Are you going through/contemplating divorce or separation?

❏ Yes   Have you recently ended or begun a new relationship?

❏ Yes   Are you having financial trouble?

Total yes responses: _____

Stressful life events vary in duration and intensity, but even one of them can put a big strain on your body and mind. If you've checked any of these, I recommend you devote some energy to lowering your stress level with the help of the techniques in chapter 10. If you've checked more than two or three, or are feeling especially stressed out, consider discussing these feelings with a qualified counselor or therapist.

Your Attitudes

Finally, let's look at some of your attitudes toward midlife issues. Some of these questions may have far-reaching implications; they're intended to get you thinking more broadly about yourself and your life. Use the space at the end of the chapter to note issues you think deserve more thought. If you like, explore these issues in your journal.

Concerning menopause:

❑ Yes ❑ No   If I could get rid of all my menopausal symptoms, my life would be fine again.

If I could get rid of all my menopausal symptoms, I would still have to worry about:

_____

When it comes to physical discomfort:
❑ I am fairly stoic/tend to minimize.
❑ I am a wimp/tend to dramatize.
❑ I simply don't have time for it: Give me a pill!

I would describe my attitude toward physical discomfort as:

_____

My personal appearance is:
❑ Very important: It's crucial to my job and/or my confidence level when interacting with other people.
❑ Somewhat important: I try to look my best, but one blemish doesn't ruin my day.
❑ Not important: Inner qualities are all that really count.

Concerning your fulfillment level:
❑ Yes ❑ No   Would you say you're "living your dream"?
❑ Yes ❑ No   Are you growing in the areas that are important to you?
❑ Yes ❑ No   Do you think your job is well suited to your talents?
❑ Yes ❑ No   Does what you do every day contribute to your happiness?
❑ Yes ❑ No   Do you feel it benefits others?

Concerning where you're at developmentally:

☐ Yes ☐ No Do you have long-range goals for your life?

☐ Yes ☐ No Are you on track for those goals?

☐ Yes ☐ No Are you in any situations (job or relationships) that are holding you back?

What do you think are your biggest areas of stress/dissatisfaction as you approach midlife?

_____

List some of your strengths: (supportive spouse, fulfilling jobs, etc.)

_____

List some of your best personal qualities: (sense of humor, discipline, problem solving, empathy, etc.)

_____

Summary

Personal points that I need to examine further, based on these questions:
(What thoughts did answering these questions raise?)

Questions for my doctor, based on these tests:

It's All About You

Each woman's experience of menopause is unique, based on her genetics, lifestyle, and beliefs. *Who you are* will determine your experience. The better you understand the hormonal, physical, and psychological pieces of your midlife puzzle, the easier it'll be to make sense of them when they're all tossed in the air together—and then, to put them together to form a *new* picture.

CHAPTER 4

Taking Control of Short-Term Symptoms

I'm drowning in stress.
I'm screaming at my kids.
My sex life has dried up.
My relationship with my husband is strained to the breaking point.
I can't remember what I was thinking from one moment to the next.
I haven't had a good night's sleep in 2 weeks.
My skin looks old.
I've put on 25 lbs.
I'm a human hotplate.
All my emotions are magnified.
I look like hell, I feel like hell, and most of the time
I just don't recognize myself.
—Excerpts from Internet chatboards.

Scary. That's the only word for it. As in the chatboard litany above, the symptoms of menopause tend to snowball, until they seem to take over your life. That's why the first order of business is to regain control by taking charge of your symptoms.

In this chapter, we'll discuss the role of lifestyle changes in relieving some of the common symptoms of perimenopause and menopause. Remember that many of these aggravating symptoms start while you're still having periods but your hormone levels are fluctuating. I'll also present various herbal and dietary remedies that many women have found to be safe and effective at reducing discomfort.

Many women find relief from short-term symptoms through lifestyle and herbal therapies alone. Others—either because their symptoms are

ASK YOUR DOCTOR

HRT AND LONG-TERM HEALTH

It's important to understand the distinction between transient symptoms such as hot flashes and mood swings—which, while inconvenient, are not health hazards—and long-term risks of heart disease, osteoporosis, and cognitive function loss. In the short term, the criteria is *whatever works for you.* While hormone replacement therapy can be very effective at reducing short-term symptoms, even strong advocates of HRT agree that a woman may reasonably choose to rely on lifestyle and alternative therapies *for symptom relief.* The real debate over HRT focuses on the issue of long-term health, where, for many women, it may offer significant benefits. Regardless of how you handle menopausal symptoms, the question of whether to begin HRT for long-term health is an important one that should be weighed with your doctor's help. Risks and benefits of HRT are discussed in chapter 12.

more severe, or for other reasons—decide in favor of hormone replacement therapy. Even if HRT resolves your symptoms, it's still important to exercise and eat well. A healthy lifestyle is the foundation of optimum health and well-being.

In this chapter, we'll look at lifestyle-oriented solutions for the following common symptoms:

- Menstrual irregularities
- Hot flashes
- Sleep problems
- Mood swings
- Loss of libido
- PMS
- Vaginal changes and incontinence
- Concentration/memory problems

Special thanks to my friend Dr. Kenneth Pelletier of the Stanford School of Medicine for some of the information on herbs contained here, which appears in his book *The Best Alternative Medicine,* and to Dr. Mary Hardy, of Cedars Sinai Medical Center in Los Angeles, who specializes in botanical medicine.

Menstrual Irregularities

Like many women, I've always been able to set my watch by my menstrual cycle. I've known which would be the days of heaviest flow, and I could anticipate the bleeding right down to the last tampon. At the same time, I've come to expect cyclic changes in my energy and mood, and I keep a chart of my menstrual cycle so I can be aware of these changes when planning my schedule. In particular, I try to plan my video shoots for those days I know I'll be feeling on top of the world.

Lately, though, things have changed: That rock-solid twenty-nine day cycle is clocking in anywhere between twenty-six and thirty days. It's very disorienting!

Changing menstrual patterns are one of the hallmarks of perimenopause, and are often the first clue that we've reached that stage. About 10 percent of women stop their periods abruptly, but for most of us, menstrual irregularities begin about seven years before menopause and may take a variety of forms, all of which are normal and common:

- Your cycle may become shorter than twenty-eight days.
- Bleeding may last for more or fewer days than usual.
- Bleeding may be heavier or lighter than usual.
- You may skip periods.

Changes are usually subtle at first. Most women find their periods becoming lighter and more erratic. Such symptoms are usually not too troubling, once you adjust to the unpredictability. Heavy bleeding, however, can be very disruptive, and may be a health concern. Although the cause is usually hormonal, it can occasionally be caused by other conditions that require immediate

HERBS FOR MENOPAUSAL SYMPTOMS

For centuries, traditional cultures have used medicinal herbs to help restore and maintain health. A growing body of scientific evidence now shows that, when used correctly, certain herbal therapies can provide effective relief from hormonally related symptoms such as hot flashes, mood swings, PMS, fatigue, and sleep problems. *Herbs should not be considered a first-line defense against long-term health risks associated with menopause.*

To get the greatest benefit, I recommend consulting a specialist who can make recommendations based on your symptoms and health history. Plants can be powerful medicines. If you have medical conditions such as high blood pressure, diabetes, or irregular heartbeat, or if you're taking a prescription medication, it's important to have someone knowledgeable advise you to avoid any adverse reactions. HRT, birth control pills, blood-thinning medication, and other prescription drugs may react negatively with herbs. I myself go to a holistic M.D.; however, a certified herbalist, naturopathic doctor, or a specialist in Chinese medicine will be able to prescribe formulas and doses that are appropriate for your needs and conditions. You should always consult a specialist before undertaking any herbal program.

Herbs shouldn't be relied upon to treat serious medical conditions such as osteoporosis and heart disease. For someone who already has thinning bones or a high risk for heart disease, conventional HRT or other medications are likely to be a better option. On the other hand, herbs can provide a good alternative for women who are perimenopausal, are starting to feel symptoms, and are not candidates for HRT or feel that HRT is too risky.

If you decide to experiment with herbal solutions on your own, be prepared to do a little homework. Herbal products are not as strictly regulated in the United States as prescription drugs, so you have to check carefully to be sure you're getting the product and dose you want. Again, finding a health care provider—whether in traditional or conventional medicine—to advise you is the safest and most effective route.

medical attention. Other causes may include benign growths called fibroids or polyps, certain birth control products, pregnancy, infections, and, in a small percentage of cases, various cancers. You should always see your doctor if you experience unusual bleeding, especially heavy bleeding, or if your periods last longer than seven days or occur more often than every twenty-one days. Spotting between periods, bleeding after intercourse, or *any* bleeding after menopause should also be reported to your doctor.

Heavy Bleeding

Heavy bleeding (of hormonal origin) occurs when you have a cycle in which no egg is released, and estrogen is allowed to build up the uterine lining unchecked by progesterone. The lining becomes thicker than usual, causing a heavier flow when it sheds.

Lifestyle Remedies

- Have your doctor check you for signs of anemia.
- Take iron supplements—very heavy periods can cause iron deficiency that may require supplementation.
- Drink plenty of fluids.
- Avoid alcohol, aspirin, and hot showers or baths—alcohol and aspirin both reduce the ability of the blood to clot, while hot showers or baths dilate blood vessels and can increase bleeding.
- Avoid the herbs black cohosh and dong quai, which can cause heavy bleeding.

Herbal Remedies

Vitex (Chaste Tree)
Vitex (Chaste Tree) is often prescribed by herbalists to regulate hormone levels in women with heavy periods. A typical dose is 20 drops of tincture once or twice daily for several months.

Flaxseed Oil

This oil is another commonly recommended supplement for preventing flooding and normalizing heavy periods. Typical doses vary from 1 to 2 tablespoons per day. Flaxseed must be kept fresh; store it in the refrigerator.

Wild Yam Root

Wild Yam Root contains substances from which synthetic hormones (including progesterone) are made and may help relieve heavy bleeding from hormonal imbalance if taken for the two weeks before your period. A typical dose is 20 drops of tincture daily.

Hot Flashes and Night Sweats

If you find you're always the one asking whether it's "hot in here," you're not alone. Hot flashes, or flushes, are the classic emblem of menopause, and, in this country at least, they affect up to 80 percent of all women.

A hot flash happens when the part of your brain that regulates body temperature gets the mistaken idea that you're too hot. In response, your body follows its normal procedure for cooling itself, exactly as it would if you *were* overheated: Your heart rate speeds up, your face turns red as blood moves toward the skin's surface, and you may break out in a sweat. Hot flashes are often followed by a chill, as your body temperature stabilizes again.

Every woman tends to have her own pattern of flashes. These can vary enormously, but they average about three and a half minutes, and usually happen three to four times a day.

Although scientists don't know exactly how, hot flashes are related to fluctuating levels of estrogen. They typically occur during the perimenopausal years, and taper off during the three years after menopause. If your ovaries are surgically removed, you'll probably start having hot flashes right away, and they may be more severe than those accompanying natural menopause.

Thankfully, my own hot flashes have been mild. Because my body has always tended to be cold, I sometimes even enjoy the little surges of warmth. My cheeks get rosy; I look in the mirror and think: "I look so healthy!" I just strip down to a tank top and make a little herbal iced tea. But I know that not all women are so lucky. Hot flashes are the main reason for a drop in well-being during perimenopause.

Hot flashes can cause:

- Embarrassment
- Poor sleep
- Stress and irritability

Night sweats are hot flashes that happen while you're sleeping. At their worst, they can be a real trial; some women awaken drenched with sweat and have to change sheets and clothing several times a night. Even worse are the effects of lost sleep on your energy, mood, and concentration. Even if nighttime flashes are not severe enough to wake you, they can still upset your natural sleep rhythms and make you more tired during the day.

Lifestyle Remedies

Hot flashes may be triggered by a variety of factors, although sometimes they seem to occur for no reason at all. Keeping a hot-flash diary for a few weeks may help you identify at least a few of your triggers and, with luck, help you reduce the frequency of your flashes. Common triggers include:

- A warm car, hot shower or bath, sauna, warm bed, or any warm environment
- Stressful situations
- Heavy or restrictive clothing
- Confined spaces
- Spicy ethnic foods, or hot meals that might raise your body temperature, like hot soup
- Coffee and tea drinks (even hot decaffeinated drinks)
- Alcohol

As you can see, hot flash triggers tend to be things that would make anyone feel a little warm—except, when you're perimenopausal, your body is far more sensitive to them.

The first line of defense against hot flashes is to address the triggers. This means dressing in layers; switching from steaming lattés to iced herbal drinks; using breathable 100 percent cotton bedding and sleepwear; and reducing your stress through progressive relaxation, yoga, meditation, or other means, some of which are discussed in chapter 10.

Meanwhile, inventive women have developed dozens of strategies for keeping their cool: Portable spritz fans, for instance, combine a spritzer bottle with a handheld fan. Some women install a ceiling fan over their bed. One woman I know soaks her socks in water before wearing them to bed: The water evaporates as she sleeps and helps keep her cool. In general, turning down the thermostat will help, especially at night. In *Dr. Susan Love's Hormone Book*, the author cites a 1992 study from the *Journal of Thermal Biology* in which women experienced fewer and less intense hot flashes in a sixty-eight-degree Fahrenheit room than one that was eighty-six degrees.

Exercise can play a major role in improving your overall sense of well-being and promoting better sleep. There is even some evidence that women who exercise frequently are less troubled by hot flashes than women who do not.

Dietary and Herbal Remedies

Soy

Isoflavones in soy protein have an estrogenlike effect that may decrease hot-flash frequency and severity up to 40 percent. A typical dose is 40 grams of soy protein per day from food sources or supplements. See chapter 11 for more information about soy and other phytoestrogens.

Black Cohosh (Remifemin)

A favorite herbal remedy of Native Americans, black cohosh, also called squawroot, is the most widely used natural alternative to HRT. Numerous studies have demonstrated its effectiveness at treating menopausal symptoms. It appears to act to normalize hormone levels, exhibiting some of the properties of estrogen. It does not offer protection against heart disease or osteoporosis, however. Although it appears to be a very safe herb, practitioners recommend using it for no more than six months. A standard dose is 2 to 4 milligrams of the active ingredient 27-deoxyaceteine per day.

Vitamin E

Four hundred International Units or more of vitamin E daily may provide relief from hot flashes, when taken for at least two to six weeks. Don't take more than 1,200 IU daily.

Dong Quai

Frequently used to treat hot flashes, dong quai is best prescribed by an herbalist, who will typically mix it with other traditional herbs in a customized formula designed to suit your needs and physiology. Discontinue if heavy menstrual bleeding develops. Dong quai should not be taken during pregnancy, and may cause photosensitivity. Don't use it if you have fibroids, nor with any blood-thinning medications.

Vitex (Chaste Tree)

Vitex is often prescribed by herbalists to regulate hormone levels in women experiencing hot flashes. A typical dose is 20 drops of tincture once or twice daily for several months.

Sleep Problems

As a child, I had no problem sleeping through the noise of freight trains and marching bands, jet planes and alarm clocks. For most of my adult life, too, I've been able to drop off immediately and fall into the most wonderful slumber. Lately, though, all bets are off. Whether it's due to hormones, family pressures, or something I ate, 3 A.M. often finds me staring at the ceiling in frustration, knowing I'll be a bleary-eyed wreck the next day.

About half the time, I'm able to get back to sleep using some of my favorite relaxation techniques. At other times, though, I lose those precious hours and pay the price. Sleep deprivation can account for many of the symptoms we associate with menopause, including:

- Irritability
- Fatigue
- Low sex drive
- Lowered resistance to stress or infection
- Headaches
- Poor concentration

It's one symptom your doctor may not ask you about, but according to the National Sleep Foundation, peri- and postmenopausal women have twice as much trouble sleeping as younger women.

Whether hormonal changes actually *cause* insomnia is not certain. Clearly, hot flashes and night sweats can turn sleep into an exhausting ordeal. Even if they're not severe enough to wake you, they can disrupt your sleep rhythm and make it less restful. Nonhormonal factors may also contribute: Sleep disturbances increase with age in both sexes, due to physical ailments, breathing problems, lower activity levels, and, especially, worry.

Although people's sleep needs vary, most of us need at least seven and a half to eight hours of sleep a night to feel refreshed, alert, and in good spirits.

There are two basic requirements for good sleep: relaxing the body, and clearing the mind. In chapter 10, you'll find my meditation and yoga routines for relaxation, which can also be very helpful for clearing your mind before bedtime.

Lifestyle Remedies

Sleep Habits and Schedule
Developing better sleep habits and establishing more of a schedule can be effective in improving sleep. Here are some suggestions that may be helpful:

- Establish a regular sleeping schedule. Go to bed at the same time every night if you can, but even if you can't, wake up at the same time every morning.
- When you can't fall asleep within twenty minutes, get up and do something relaxing. Don't try to go to sleep again until you feel sleepy. Use your bedroom only for activities that promote relaxation.
- Take naps. Napping can help repay your sleep debt and make your days more productive. According to William Dement, M.D., director of the Stanford University Sleep Disorders Center, about 90 percent of us become sleepy or tired in the early afternoon, around two o'clock. (And you thought it was just you!) Since it's easier to sleep when you're sleepy, that's a great time to catch up. A half-hour nap can restore mental alertness for up to six hours.

Relaxing

Destressing before bedtime—and throughout the day—will help you fall asleep more easily and sleep more soundly. Here are some suggestions:

- Relax *before* getting into bed, by curling up with a good book, listening to soft music, doing progressive relaxation exercises such as the one described in chapter 10, meditating, making love—whatever works for you.
- A hot bath before bedtime can be relaxing—but be aware that it can be a hot-flash trigger as well.
- A good self-administered foot massage right before bedtime is a great way to relax.
- Try to determine what keeps you from sleeping. Is it certain foods? It is unresolved anger or anxiety? Keep a record of triggers.
- Defuse any "ticking bombs." Don't wait until 11 P.M. (or 3 A.M.!) to address issues that may disrupt your sleep—learn to recognize them earlier in the day. Try to deal with them and let go of them as they come up.

Exercise

Both strength training and aerobic exercise have been shown to improve sleep. Don't overexert immediately before bedtime, however. If possible, try to exercise no later than the early evening. Stretching exercises or certain yoga postures, however, done just before going to bed can be very useful for relaxing muscle tension.

Your Environment

Examine your acoustical environment. Are there noises from traffic, neighbors, or other sources that may be keeping you awake? Try using earplugs or some type of masking sound, such as an electric fan or white noise generator. Some people are lulled to sleep by soothing ambient noise. Examine the entire bedroom environment: Is your mattress comfortable? Would lowering the temperature of your bedroom or installing a ceiling fan over the bed help you sleep? Is your sleepwear or bedding trapping perspiration and causing you to sweat more? Would making your room darker (or less dark, using a low-wattage night-light) help you feel more relaxed?

Drugs

Avoid stimulants. Depending on your tolerance, it's best to forgo any caffeine at least six hours before bedtime. Besides coffee and tea, other sources of caffeine include soft drinks, chocolate, and some types of aspirin. Nicotine and various over-the-counter cold medications and diet aids can have a stimulant effect as well. Sleeping pills can be useful for short-term sleep problems, but they should never be used for more than two weeks. They can suppress REM sleep, interrupting the dream cycles that the brain must move through in order to stay sane. They can also produce a rebound effect, making the user unable to fall asleep at all. Finally, don't make a habit of using alcohol to fall asleep; it can disrupt normal sleep cycles and end up causing wakefulness.

Herbal Remedies

Valerian

A common herbal remedy for insomnia, valerian has a thousand-year track record as a safe and effective mild sedative and sleep aid. Unlike barbiturates and other conventional insomnia drugs, it does not interact synergistically with alcohol. Valerian may require several weeks to become effective. A typical dose is 2 to 3 grams of powdered herb, or 600 milligrams (1 to 2 milliliters) of an ethanol extract taken an hour or two before bedtime.

Mood Swings

Just this week, I was in the art room of my daughter's school, helping another mother who volunteers there as a teacher. She was setting out the art paper at the empty desks, and the task was proving too much—she was looking extremely tense and flustered. When I asked if there was anything I could do to help, she broke down and sobbed: "I really need that book you're writing!"

When people talk about "mood swings," they're usually *not* referring to elation, but rather waves of sadness or flashes of anger that seem out of proportion to the situation at hand. Minor frustrations become cataclysmic; simple tasks can seem overwhelming.

While hormonal changes at perimenopause can amplify moods just as they do during a normal cycle, other perimenopausal symptoms—especially loss of sleep—can fray your nerves and lower your tolerance. That's why anything that reduces hot flashes or helps you sleep better is guaranteed to improve your mood.

Lifestyle Remedies

Aerobic exercise is my number one prescription for improving mood. Exercise releases endorphins—those "feel-good" chemicals in the brain—creating a mood-heightening effect that can last for hours afterward. We've all seen how even a short walk can make a bad day bearable again. Adopting a full routine of cardio training, strength training, and healthy eating will make you feel like a different person. I also recommend limiting

DEPRESSION

An occasional bout of the blues—a depressed *mood*—is common during perimenopause; these are usually transient and require no special treatment. *Depression syndrome*, however, is an ongoing depressed mood that interferes with daily life. Women who have suffered from depression syndrome in the past are probably more likely than other women to become depressed during perimenopause, but there's no evidence that menopause causes depression syndrome in women who are not prone to it.

your consumption of sugar, caffeine, and alcohol, and using stress-reducing techniques such as progressive relaxation and yoga, which are both described in chapter 10.

And for those out-of-control, sad-or-mad moments, here are some coping strategies from psychologist Ann Christie, Ph.D.

For Overreacting

Let's say the store clerk is ignoring you, or traffic makes you five minutes late to work. Is it reason to blow a fuse or burst into tears? If it is, says Ann, you've gotten way too caught up in the minutiae. Step back and ask yourself: *How big a deal is this, really? On a ten-point scale—ten being a major earthquake—where would this fall?* For me, most of life's irritations only rate about half a point. Once I realize that, I'm usually able to let them go.

For Uncontrolled Crying

Remember the old melodramas where someone slaps the hysterical woman in the face to calm her down? A similar, but gentler, approach works just as well. If you find yourself unable to stop crying at an inconvenient time, go into the bathroom, hold your palms under the cold water, and press the water to your face. The coldness against your skin will provide a little shock to your system, which should change your mental state and bring you back to the present. Later, try the technique called *controlled crying,* described in chapter 10.

Herbal Remedies

Kava Kava

In his book *The Best Alternative Medicine,* Stanford researcher Dr. Kenneth Pelletier cites several studies showing that kava kava may help reduce anxiety and induce sleep. Kava should not be used with alcohol or other antidepressants, and it should not be taken for more than three months at a time. Other practitioners suggest that kava kava may also be helpful in treating menstrual cramps. Standard typical dosage is 45 to 70 milligrams of kavalactone.

St. John's Wort

Dr. Pelletier calls this herb "one of the powerhouses of contemporary herbal medicine," and it's frequently used for reducing anxiety and depression, and promoting restful sleep. According to Pelletier, doctors in Germany now prescribe it more frequently than Prozac. St. John's wort should not be taken long term or with other antidepressants. A typical dosage is 300 to 400 milligrams of the extract, containing 0.3 percent of the active ingredient hypericin. Allow several weeks to see an effect.

Loss of Libido

One of the first things women (and men!) always want to know is: *Will menopause change our sex life?* While there are some encouraging statistics about women whose enjoyment of sex seems to blossom at menopause, the reality is that many women do experience a decline in drive. A loss of sexual interest may be caused by a combination of factors, including physical symptoms that sap your energy or make sex uncomfortable, stress, relationship issues, and hormonal changes.

Lifestyle Remedies

Because the causes of a low libido may be manifold, the solution, too, may end up being a combined program of sorts—pelvic exercise to improve vaginal health, use of lubricants or moisturizers, additional foreplay, and better communication with your partner. Often, just a new dedication to general health and well-being will start a chain reaction that gets you feeling frisky again. Testosterone is sometimes prescribed to increase libido—although little research has been done on its safety and effectiveness. Libido and other sexual concerns are discussed in detail in chapter 6.

Herbal and Dietary Remedies

Ginkgo Biloba

Recent research suggests ginkgo biloba may stimulate libido with relatively few side effects. In a pilot study at the University of California at

San Francisco, ginkgo reversed sexual problems in 84 percent of men and women who were taking antidepressant drugs such as Prozac. A larger trial is under way.

DHEA

According to a 1999 German study published in the *New England Journal of Medicine,* DHEA supplements were found to relieve depression and anxiety and improve sexual health in women with adrenal insufficiency. The women taking DHEA had more frequent sexual thoughts and fantasies and their sexual interest improved. *Caution:* The effectiveness and safety of over-the-counter DHEA supplements have not been clinically verified. There may be adverse side effects or risks associated with their use. Consult your doctor before taking any DHEA supplements.

Vaginal Changes and Incontinence

Decreasing levels of estrogen cause changes in the vagina and urethra that can impair lubrication and make intercourse painful, while increasing the chance of urinary tract infections. Over time, the muscles of the pelvic floor may lose their tone. It may become difficult to control the flow of urine, and some leakage may occur when laughing, coughing, or sneezing, or during intercourse.

Lifestyle Remedies

Regular sexual activity will help keep the vagina lubricated, and Kegel exercises can help keep the surrounding muscles toned. Water-based lubricants such as Astroglide or K-Y Jelly will help during intercourse, and other moisturizers such as Replens can be used regularly to restore vaginal moisture. These solutions and others are covered in detail in chapter 6.

Herbal and Dietary Remedies

Oatmeal Baths and Vitamin E Oil

Oatmeal baths or vitamin E oil applied directly to the vaginal tissue may help relieve itching or irritation.

Yogurt

Eating yogurt or acidophilus capsules may improve pH balance and reduce bacterial infections and irritation. Yogurt is not a treatment for dryness.

Soy

Isoflavones in soy protein have an estrogenlike effect that may improve vaginal dryness. A typical dose is 40 grams of soy protein per day from food sources or supplements. See chapter 11 for more information about soy and other phytoestrogens.

PMS

Although many women experience PMS throughout their reproductive years, PMS that begins or becomes worse in your late thirties may be a symptom of perimenopause. Typical symptoms of PMS are breast tenderness, bloating, weight gain, depression, anxiety, irritability, and sleep problems occurring on a monthly basis.

What if you don't know if what you're experiencing is PMS? Keeping a menstrual calendar can help determine how much your symptoms vary with your cycle. Some researchers believe women who've battled PMS over the years may have a more difficult time at menopause.

Lifestyle Remedies

A basic lifestyle prescription for PMS is one aimed at general health and well-being: It consists of regular exercise and a balanced diet that includes adequate amounts of the B vitamins, vitamin C, vitamin E, calcium, magnesium, and zinc. (See chapter 11 for more detailed nutritional guidelines.) In a 1994 study by Dr. Julie A. Aganoff of the University of Queensland in Australia, PMS sufferers who exercised regularly improved their concentration, disposition, and discomfort. Dr. D. Yvonne Jones of the National Cancer Institute found that women on a low-fat diet (less than 20 percent of calories) had significantly fewer physical PMS symptoms.

Look for triggers in your diet: Some women find that their symptoms are made worse by foods such as sugar, red meat, dairy products, salt, caffeine, and alcohol. Follow your symptoms for several months, and keep a record of what you're eating. Maintaining a consistent blood sugar level by limiting sweet snacks and desserts may help even out symptoms.

Herbal Remedies

Dong Quai

Frequently used to treat hot flashes, dong quai can also be used for PMS; in this case, it's taken from day fourteen until menstruation. Discontinue if heavy menstrual bleeding develops. Dong quai should not be taken during pregnancy, and it may cause photosensitivity. Don't use it if you have fibroids, and don't take it with any blood-thinning medications. Dong quai is best prescribed by an herbalist, who will typically mix it with other traditional herbs in a customized formula designed to suit your needs and physiology.

Evening Primrose Oil

Although it has not clearly been proven to relieve PMS symptoms generally, several studies have shown that evening primrose oil, which contains essential fatty acids, can help specifically relieve breast pain associated with PMS. A typical dose is 2 to 4 grams (containing 9 percent gamma-linolenic acid). Some researchers believe you can get similar benefits from other sources of essential fatty acids, such as fish oils or flaxseed.

Vitex (Chaste Tree)

Vitex is often prescribed by herbalists to regulate hormone levels in women with PMS. A typical dose would be 20 drops of tincture once or twice daily for several months.

Concentration and Memory

Fuzzy thinking, difficulty concentrating, and short-term memory loss are all ways of describing the mental fog that often comes over perimenopausal women. *Where did I put my keys? What was his name again? Why did I come into this room?* Fuzzy thinking is usually a temporary symptom, but it can be a disturbing one, especially if you work in a job that demands mental sharpness.

Most authorities agree that short-term memory loss is due to aging, along with stress and lack of sleep. As you get older, it takes longer to access information you've stored away. This is normal. It doesn't mean you're developing Alzheimer's, or are any more likely to.

That's not to say hormones aren't involved, however. Research has shown that hormonal changes during a normal cycle can have a subtle effect on how well we think. In addition, some studies have shown that women taking HRT do slightly better on tests designed to assess their mental function. This could mean that women who are not suffering from hot flashes and lack of sleep are in a better frame of mind to concentrate. Or it may mean that estrogen has a slight beneficial effect on mental function. Still, men experience memory problems with age, too. Whatever effect hormones may be having on your ability to think clearly, it's hard to separate it from the effects of worry, lack of sleep, and other stresses of midlife. Sleep deprivation, in particular, can have a huge impact on mood and memory, as anyone who has ever cared for a newborn can attest. Memory or concentration problems can also be an indication of depression.

Lifestyle Remedies

Sugar

I know that if I eat too much sugar, I practically start forgetting my own name. So if I'm working on a project or giving a speech, I have to be very careful about what sort of sugary treats I indulge in. Response to sugar is an individual phenomenon; I recommend tracking your consumption of refined sweets against your symptoms to learn whether sugar affects you in this way.

Vitamins and Minerals

Low levels of vitamin E in elderly patients have been associated with memory problems. Taking 400 to 800 IU of vitamin E per day may protect brain cells by guarding against damage from free radicals.

Many nutrients are important for good brain functions. You can rule out the possibility of vitamin or mineral deficiencies by making sure you get the required daily amounts of the major nutrients, preferably from a balanced diet. See chapter 11 for more nutritional guidelines.

Aerobic Exercise

In a study at the University of Illinois, participants ranging from age fifty to seventy-five improved their cognitive abilities by walking three times a week for fifteen to forty-five minutes. Aerobic exercise improves circulation, bringing more oxygen to the brain.

Good Dietary Habits

Eating regularly and avoiding extreme calorie restriction will aid mental function. In a study reported in the *American Journal of Epidemiology,* poor dietary habits, such as skipping meals or eating too little, tripled the number of people suffering from memory problems.

Herbal Remedies

Ginkgo Biloba

Commonly used in Europe to treat memory problems and mood disorders, ginkgo biloba appears to have proven generally effective in a limited number of trials. The recommended dose is 40 milligrams three times a day for at least four to six weeks. Minor side effects can occur, so check with an herbalist or read the accompanying literature carefully.

Other Symptoms

Other, less common, symptoms are sometimes reported around menopause, including:

- Muscle and joint pains
- Migraines
- Crawling skin

- Heart palpitations
- Dry skin
- Fatigue

As with the major symptoms, some of these are probably related to hormonal changes, while others may be age or stress related. Whatever their origin, the lifestyle and alternative remedies listed in this chapter will help. Two other remedies that may be helpful are ginseng and behavioral treatments.

Ginseng for Fatigue

Ginseng has a long history of traditional use in China, primarily as a tonic. The concept of a tonic herb—one that supports normal function over a long period of time—is not one we generally use in this country. In low doses, however, ginseng may be helpful in combating fatigue and increasing endurance, restoring energy and providing a more positive outlook. Because it may have a stimulant effect in some people, it's not recommended for sleep disturbances. There are many different ginseng varieties available; Chinese medicine uses up to seven different types. Ginseng can have side effects, including high blood pressure and uterine bleeding—if you experience these, you should stop taking it or reduce the dosage. To make sure you're getting the best product for you, it's a good idea to consult with a traditional or holistic doctor or an herbalist.

Behavioral Treatments for Headache

The U.S. Headache Consortium reviewed more than 355 studies that looked at nondrug treatments of migraine and found that among the most helpful were mediation, yoga, self-hypnosis, and biofeedback.

How to Get Started

Herbal remedies tend to be very mild in their effects. Except where noted, the herbs listed here are compatible with each other and may be used in combination. Nevertheless, I recommend working with your doctor and experimenting one at a time with any herbs aimed at the same symptoms; that way, you'll be able to accurately judge the results. Many herbs can require several weeks or months to achieve an effect, so experimentation does take patience. Still, being willing to experiment is the key, since everyone's body is different. Always tell your doctor *everything* you're taking—whether it's vitamin and mineral supplements, herbs, or estrogenic foods. Meanwhile, follow the exercise, dietary, and stress-reduction recommendations throughout this book to help improve your general health and increase your overall vitality. Doing so is the best first line of defense against menopausal symptoms.

I am unsettled.
I wonder who I will be.
I hear voices of the future.
I see an intersection in my life.
I want to be everything.
I am open.

I pretend to be unshakable.
I feel frail.
I touch dreams.
I cry for wisdom.
I am human.

I contemplate life's struggles.
I say why me?
I dream of prosperity and happiness.
I try to stay true to my dreams.
I hope to find my calling.
I am unsettled . . . but not for long.

—Kate Grace, age twelve

Chapter 5
Your Inner Self

My daughter Kate recently shared this poem with me. Like many mothers, I'll be hitting menopause around the same time my girls reach puberty. Reading her poem, I'm amazed at how relevant my twelve-year-old daughter's words are to the growing pangs of midlife.

For many women, menopause is a time of restlessness and reassessment. We look in the mirror and seem to see a stranger. Familiar ways of being suddenly lack meaning, and we struggle to get a positive handle on our future. Although women's menopausal journeys are as individual as the women themselves, there's a common pattern:

- The one–two punch of midlife stress and hormonal symptoms
- The realization that you've reached a major life marker
- A cascade of fears about getting older
- A feeling of being lost, and a need to reinvent your life from the ground up.

Would you believe me if I said all this was a good thing? Well, it can be. The reassessment that takes place gives us a fresh chance at having the life we want. Even the edgy emotional undercurrents can be channeled in positive ways, providing the energy to throw out the old and reach for something new.

A New Era

I was delighted recently to read about a forty-five-year-old woman who started her own travel company, organizing tours for menopausal women. It's a great business idea, in part because it's really the perfect metaphor for midlife. Each of us, ready or not, is embarking on her own "menopausal tour." Whether it turns out to be a nightmare or a great adventure will depend in part on how well we plan for it—what we pack, and what we leave behind.

For some women, just give them a few hormones and their life is good again. But for others, issues come up that reach to the very foundations of their lives.

One of the most sobering of these, of course, is that, in losing our reproductive capability, we're saying good-bye to an entire era of our lives. The big question then becomes: *What are we getting in return? What is there to look forward to?* We hear encouraging phrases like "post-menopausal zest" or "wisdom and experience." One of the challenges of menopause is dealing with preconceptions about what it "means"—and not just your *own* preconceptions.

My friend Sandy remembers the day that, at forty-seven, with no prior symptoms, she learned from her doctor that she was menopausal. In shock, she sought the support of some close friends. Instead of sympathy, she struck a brick wall of denial. "They didn't want to know about it," she said. "They have this idea that menopause is going to reduce them to asexual blobs, or turn them into their grandmothers overnight."

These fears made them incapable of supporting their friend. "They avoided me like I was a ghost," Sandy told me in disbelief. "Like they were afraid if they touched me they would catch it." To them, menopause meant *old.*

In our youth-hungry culture, the slightest hint we're getting older is terrifying. In our minds, it's a fast trip from being a woman of "a certain age" to being simply an old woman—when in fact anything remotely resembling "old" is still decades away.

The truth is, fifty is a kind of magic age—a time when you really can have it all: experience and wisdom, along with strength and vitality. Being *just mature enough* to have an interesting take on things, yet still energetic enough to follow your dreams—that's what the middle years are all about. Menopausal symptoms may have the floor right now, but they'll pass, and what could very well turn out to be the best decade of your life is just beginning.

Staying Centered

The other day, I overheard one of my daughter's friends complaining about her mom being on a "menopause roller coaster," and then groaning: "We can't take her *anywhere!*" (Yes, this is how twelve-year-olds are talking about their moms today!) Granted, menopause does crazy things to your moods, but it's important not to let this be a license to be a shrew. If you use menopause to excuse bad behavior, it can undermine your self-respect and damage your relationships.

Believe me, I've been there: You're feeling stressed out, and then some little thing comes along to send you right over the edge. In those situations, I always ask myself: *Is it worth it?* So my dry cleaning wasn't ready when it was supposed to be. Flying off the handle at the clerk isn't going to get the clothes clean. All it's going to do is raise my blood pressure, tax my adrenals, and spoil my mascara. Is it really worth the stress? What's more, if *I* hadn't waited until Thursday to drop off my clothes, none of this would be happening! Learn to recognize when you're slipping off balance, and do whatever you need to do to recenter. In particular, examine the ways in which you may be contributing to your stress. One effective way to do this is to take a daily inventory. I like to do this as part of my bedtime ritual:

FIND MENTORS
Seek out older women of depth and substance who have experience with midlife changes. They can help you put things in perspective. If not, at least they can help you have a good laugh—that's usually the best remedy of all!

- Evaluate your actions and decide if you need to apologize to anyone. Yes, really! Keeping your conscience clear and your relationships current will lighten your load. Don't let yourself use the excuse "Oh, I'm in menopause."
- Figure out what's causing your stress, and how to relieve it. Chances are, you're simply expecting too much of yourself at times when you're already off balance from lack of sleep or other symptoms.

I know this is a tall order when you're already short on patience. Still, taking responsibility for your stress puts you back in control— believe me, that will make you feel better!

When I become impatient and short with people, it's usually because I'm trying to do too much in too little time. If I want to do my best work *and* get the best out of the people I work with, I need to relax my schedule and give myself room to breathe. Of course, it's one thing to notice it— it's another to change it. Make the adjustment.

Other Good Strategies

Lower Your Expectations
Perfectionism is a luxury most of us can't afford. If everything in your life has to be a "ten," you're sure to be stressed and dissatisfied most of the time. If you shoot for sixes, you stand a good chance of bettering your expectations and feeling generally happier.

Try to Laugh at Yourself
Recently I was talking with a good friend, describing a stressful confrontation I'd just had. Instead of backing me up, she surprised me by saying: "Don't you realize when you act like that, people just want to lock you in a closet?" I couldn't help but laugh, and that image now makes me think twice when I'm feeling impatient or irritated.

Journal Exercise

WHAT DON'T YOU LIKE ABOUT YOUR LIFE?

Step 1.

What don't you like about your life? Set a timer for three to five minutes and make a list of all the things that are making you unhappy (your job, your teenager's friends, your weight, your relationship, your parents' health . . .). What's worrying you or weighing you down? Just keep writing until the time is up.

Step 2.

Think for a few minutes and narrow your list down to three items you think you could address in the next year.

Step 3.

Now pick one of those three items, and spend three to five minutes brainstorming possible approaches to the problem. Get past the parts you can't control and focus on the parts you can do something about.

Suppose you're having a problem with your teen, for example, and you're worried about the company he keeps. Go beyond the worry and think of constructive solutions. What can you do to foster other relationships—or to strengthen *your* relationship with your child?

Your list might read:

- Plan a day together.
- Introduce him to a new extracurricular class or youth group, where he'll be challenged and hopefully become involved.
- Try to remember everything you can about what it was like to be his age.
- Pray!

Simplifying Relationships

In packing for your midlife voyage, it's a good time to examine your relationships, to decide which will travel well and which you may need to leave behind. The older I get, the more I realize I want to be around people who share my interests and like me for who I am. Most of all, I appreciate people who share my positive attitude. Here are some possible ways you might revitalize this area of your life:

- **Take responsibility for making your interactions more rewarding, and eliminate toxic relationships where necessary.**
  Life is too short to spend in relationships that are causing you obvious grief and stress. Such truly "toxic" relationships are best eliminated. Some relationships, though, may not qualify as toxic—they may be genuine friendships that have just gotten a little lazy. In that case, when the conversation seems to turn negative or gossipy, point the finger of responsibility at yourself. Change the subject, and try to set it back on track. If it's a relationship of substance, doing so should strengthen it. As a last resort, though, you may have to spend less time with the person.
- **Learn the art of marginalizing.**
  Sometimes a person is causing you a lot of grief by persisting in addictive, abusive, or very negative behavior, but you're unable to eliminate him or her from your life because of family ties. To *marginalize* means to lovingly, but firmly, move that person out of the center of things. It's wonderful how this takes the heat off! Although you reserve a place for the person in your life, it's far enough out on the margin that the emotional charge is diffused.

  I've worked hard to do this with my husband. For various reasons, we decided it is in our family's best interest for us to separate; however, he remains an important part of our lives. While we continue to act as close partners in raising our daughters, the extra distance relieves me of feeling overly attached and reactive. I don't mean to suggest that such a process is ever easy or clear-cut. It's a balancing act that, for our daughters' sake, is well worth the effort.

Marginalizing is a good approach to try with anything that you decide is no longer central to your well-being.

- **Stop trying to control everything.**

If you're prone to fretting over every detail of the lives of those you're close to—give yourself a break and learn how to stop controlling people! Stop worrying about whether your kids pierce their ears or wear purple with pink. Let go of the small stuff. The minute you do, you'll feel lighter.

The Search for Meaning

As that beautiful passage from the book of Ecclesiastes reminds us, there are seasons to life—a time for every purpose under Heaven. Typically, the first two decades of our adulthood are spent in the trenches: getting an education, starting a business, raising a family. But at some time in our forties or fifties, most of us take note of the lengthening shadows and begin—or intensify—our search for *meaning*.

This is the spiritual season—the time for asking yourself: *What are my causes? My passions?* Your spiritual quest may be outward or inward looking. It may or may not be religious in the strict sense. The point is to work from your own definition of spirituality, of meaning—however you may conceive of it. There's no question more basic than *Why am I here?* And if this isn't the time to give it serious consideration, when is?

Some Specific Tips

Address "If Only's"

Make a list of things you've always wanted to do but haven't made time for. Include everything you can think of, big and small—things to do, places to go, classes, hobbies to try, games to play, old friends to look up, the books you've wanted to read. Keep adding to it as you think of new things. Then pick one and plan how you'll go about doing it.

Explore Creative Outlets

Creative activities bring your true self to light right before your eyes. A hundred years ago, women got together to make beautiful quilts and embroidered linens. In doing so, they enjoyed fellowship _and_ self-expression. You can do the same. Sign up for a pottery class, sing in a choir, join a writing group.

Identify "Aha!" Moments

Now and then, we all have moments when the lightbulb above our head goes on. It could be a new insight, a solution to a problem, or an inkling of a possible new direction. Watch for these moments: They're the path of bread crumbs your soul leaves for you—and they can lead to places of great fulfillment.

Living on the Edge

"Think positively!" says the pamphlet your doctor hands you. "A positive attitude will help you take control of your future!"

I don't know about you, but when I feel like I'm swimming in stress, a positive attitude can be hard to muster. Fortunately, menopause comes with its _own_ attitude. It's a kind of urgency, an edge. This is the lifeline it throws you. The menopausal "edge" has a wonderful way of cutting to the truth of who you are—_if_ you let that happen.

Listen to my friend Lee's story:

> By the time I reached perimenopause, I had been working in the same office for more than fifteen years and I was miserable. I knew I needed out, but I had no idea what I would do. One day I simply exploded in a full-blown anxiety attack—and I decided then to give notice. It was the best thing I've ever done. The anxiety disappeared immediately. Within a few months, I started my own business as a professional organizer. My whole life changed. I feel inspired by life instead of drained by it.

Lee had known she needed a change for a long time, but it was the stress of perimenopause that pushed her on to a bright future.

That's how it works. Menopause wrestles with you: It takes away your patience for compromise, it wears away your ability to keep your life on hold—until finally, *you no longer have the strength to hold yourself back*. You let go, and you find yourself flying to where your dreams want to take you.

And so, as my daughters and I each stand on the brink of our respective transformations, I tell myself what I would tell them: The turbulence of the hormonal transition will pass. Meanwhile, let the journey be an adventure. Be grateful for the uncertainty you feel, for *uncertainty* is just another name for *possibility*.

Chapter 6

Sexual Health

One of the questions women always ask is what effect menopause will have on their sex life. Sex is a curiously complex and deeply personal force in our lives. This makes it one of the most important—and tricky—areas affected by midlife changes.

Any woman who truly wants to maintain an active and satisfying sex life can do so. But it can take work, and maybe a little soul searching. This chapter will offer tips and strategies for overcoming physical problems that interfere with good sex, and provide diet and exercise suggestions that may help. But the real issues are often psychological, social, and interpersonal. How you feel about sex, how you expect sex to be at midlife, what sort of relationship you have with your partner—all these matter more than the hormonal changes at menopause.

When it comes to things like sexual interest or frequency, there's no one standard. I know young, single women whose lives virtually revolve around boyfriends and sex. But by midlife, aging, marriage, and having kids may change the picture. Some women, for a variety of reasons, are most comfortable *without* a sexual relationship in their lives—

and that's fine. Others may use midlife as a chance to explore their sexuality more fully.

However you may feel about sex, though, I urge you to see your sexuality as an important aspect of health and vitality. It is one of the body's systems. Even if you have decided not to engage in sex with a partner, it's vital to maintain the health of your urogenital system—just as you would that of your heart, lungs, or muscles.

The Changes

Most women report some change in sexual function at menopause. Surveys show that women typically have fewer sexual thoughts, experience poorer lubrication, and may feel less satisfied with their partners as lovers. Frequency of intercourse often declines, and some studies show a correlation between this and declining levels of testosterone. Other changes may occur, too, such as decreased arousal and ability to orgasm.

The good news is that for many women, the changes are mild, and the majority of women report feeling satisfied with their sex lives after menopause. How *you* feel about any changes you experience depends on you, and your attitudes about sex. How you'll solve them depends on the exact mix of factors causing them.

Let's look at some of the factors that may affect sexual health during midlife.

Vaginal Problems

Loss of estrogen causes the vagina to become shorter and narrower, and lose some of its elasticity. Blood supply and secretions decrease, and the vagina doesn't lubricate as well during sex. The once succulent inner walls may become tissue-thin and dry. Intercourse can become uncomfortable or even painful. The thinner vaginal walls are also more vulnerable to infection.

Urinary Problems

At the same time that the vaginal walls are shrinking, the muscles around the vagina and urethra begin to lose volume and strength. It may become difficult to control the flow of urine, and some leakage may occur when laughing, coughing, or sneezing, or during intercourse. This is called stress incontinence, and it affects up to 30 percent of women between the ages of fifty and sixty-four.

In addition, various other physical, chemical, and lifestyle factors may enter the picture:

- Menopausal symptoms such as hot flashes or irritability
- Disease or chronic pain, such as low back or neck pain
- Stress
- Fatigue
- Antidepressants
- Age-related changes (not associated with hormones) such as body image or general health
- Changes in your partner's health or ability to perform
- Relationship problems

Ultimately, though, your values and priorities have the greatest influence in determining the role of sex in your life. How important is sex to your overall enjoyment of life? Do you have negative feelings toward it, or preconceptions about what sex after menopause is likely to be? If you're someone who likes sex a lot, and even *counts* on it as an important source of validation, release, or pleasure, then a drop in frequency and desire may motivate you to find creative ways to keep your sex life active. On the other hand, if frequent sex is not central to your well-being, a slightly downsized sex life may feel fine to you. What's more, if sex has been unsatisfying for some time or is associated with feelings of obligation or other negative emotions, you may actually be relieved to let it go. For you, the fact that you feel fewer sexual urges or imagine that people no longer see you as a sexual being may be a wonderful, liberating feeling. *Note:* While maintaining a sex *life* is optional, maintaining good sexual *health* is still important.

Exercise, Diet, and Lifestyle Solutions for Vaginal Health

Whether or not you wish to maintain an active sex life, I strongly believe in preserving the health and vitality of the sexual organs. Like other systems in the body, they, too, operate on the "use it or lose it" principle. According to Masters and Johnson, regular sexual stimulation at least once or twice a week (either with a partner or through masturbation) will improve blood flow and help maintain muscle tone and lubrication. Of course, commonsense rules apply: If penetration is uncomfortable, use a commercial lubricant, go slow and easy, and avoid excessive thrusting.

In addition, narrowing of the vaginal opening may cause painful intercourse if you don't have sex frequently. Nonsexual stimulation through the use of a medical dilator is another option. These are plastic rods of varying sizes designed to be inserted in the vagina and held there for approximately ten minutes, two to three times a week, to stretch the tissue. Available from medical supply stores, dilators are especially recommended to prevent scar tissue forming if you've had internal radiation therapy.

Pelvic Exercise

Kegels are exercises that tone and strengthen the *pubococcygius,* or PC muscle—the muscle surrounding the opening of the vagina. A strong PC muscle is vital to the health of the reproductive organs. Like any other muscle in the body, the PC muscle needs regular exercise to remain firm, especially after childbirth or menopause. When done correctly, "Kegeling" can alleviate up to 90 percent of stress incontinence and heighten pleasure and sensitivity during intercourse.

You can find your PC muscle by tightening the vaginal opening, as if you were stopping the flow of urine. Or you can locate the muscle by putting a finger in your vagina and squeezing until you feel the muscle tighten around your finger. Try to keep the muscles of the buttocks, thighs, and stomach as relaxed as possible.

Here's a simple, four-part routine designed to strengthen and tone the entire PC muscle:

- **Simple Squeeze**

Squeeze the PC muscle and hold for three to five seconds, then release. Relax for the same number of seconds (for instance, a three-second squeeze, followed by a three-second rest). Repeat for a total of five repetitions. Work up to ten five-second squeezes, three times per day.

- **Elevator Squeeze**

Slowly contract your PC muscle on a count of one through five, and visualize it lifting up as if there were a cord pulling it into the center of your body. Remember to keep your buttocks and abdominal muscles relaxed. Visualize your pelvic floor rising like an elevator with each count until you've reached the fifth floor, and then let it gradually relax back down, counting backward to one. At first, it may be difficult to keep the muscle lifting all the way to five. Take it up as far as you can and hold it steady for the remainder of the five seconds. Repeat five times.

- **Easy Flutter**

Squeeze for one second, relax for one second, and squeeze again. Squeeze and release ten times, just slowly enough that you can still distinguish the contraction from the release.

- **Quick Flutter**

Squeeze and release as quickly as you can without stopping. If the contraction and release start to get jumbled, focus on the contraction. In the beginning, it may feel more like a stutter than a flutter, but with time you'll be as graceful as a bird. Do ten quick repetitions.

Finish your Kegel routine with a final set of five Elevator Squeezes, slowly lifting and lowering the muscle with controlled movement.

Do the entire routine three times a day. You may want to gradually increase either the number of repetitions or the time you hold the contraction. If you don't have time to do the whole routine, make sure you do at least one set of Elevator Squeezes and one of Quick Flutters three times a day.

Vaginal Weights and Other Resistance Devices

Although Kegel exercises don't require any special equipment, some women feel they get a firmer contraction when there's something for the muscles to contract *around*. This is especially true if the muscles have already lost some strength and tone. Various devices are designed for this purpose including vaginal barbells, weights, or cones. Inserted in the vagina during Kegel sessions, they may help you focus more effectively on the target muscle. Vaginal weights are available from medical supply stores or catalogs specializing in self-care products. Talk with your doctor to decide whether these are a good option for you.

Remedies for Vaginal Irritation and Dryness

• Water-based lubricants such as Astroglide, K-Y Jelly, and others can help keep vaginal tissues moist and prevent discomfort during intercourse. Avoid oil-based products, such as Vaseline or baby oil, or products containing alcohol or perfume. Vaginal moisturizers such as Replens or K-Y Long-Lasting Vaginal Moisturizer may provide more continuous benefits than vaginal lubricants. In addition, they may also reduce the chance of infection by helping keep the vagina more acidic. Replens, which contains polycarbophil, has been shown to be about as effective as estrogen-containing creams in keeping the vagina moist and elastic; it does not actually restore vaginal tissue, however, as prescription estrogen products do.

• Try oatmeal baths. There are several commercially available oatmeal bath remedies, such as Aveeno. Simply pour a packet into a hot bath and enjoy a good soak. Alternatively, cooked oatmeal can be placed in a strainer and held under the tap.

• Vitamin E applied as a cream, oil, or suppository can help relieve itching or irritation. Break capsules open before inserting into the vagina. Always make sure your products are pure.

• Avoid antihistamines and other substances known to have a dehydrating effect, such as caffeine, alcohol, and diuretics. Drink plenty of liquids such as water, fruit juice, and herbal teas. This can help with vaginal dryness.

• Traditional Chinese herbal formulas containing roots of rehmannia and dong quai have long been used to promote vaginal moisture.

- Eating yogurt with lactobacillus acidophilus (good bacteria) or taking acidophilus capsules or powders may improve pH balance and reduce bacterial infections and vaginal irritation. Acidophilus is not an effective remedy for dryness.
- Avoid soaps, fabric softeners, and other perfumed products that may be causing an allergic reaction in the sensitive vaginal area.
- Wearing natural-fiber clothing can help relieve itching.
- Estrogenic foods such as soy may help relieve vaginal dryness.

Sex Solutions

- Educate yourself, through books and videos, about sexuality and sexual functioning.
- Realize that a satisfying and active sex life is possible at any age, and that regular sex can improve your urogenital health, self-esteem, and general well-being.
- Experiment with a different style of lovemaking, involving longer foreplay to increase lubrication and less emphasis on intercourse. Experiment with positions that reduce the force of thrusting.
- Aggressively manage symptoms that interfere with sexual enjoyment, such as vaginal dryness, hot flashes, or chronic back or neck pain.
- Seek help from a psychotherapist or sex therapist to deal with relationship problems or dysfunction, or to figure out how to work around chronic physical problems.
- Getting into shape physically should help you feel sexier. If you're getting into shape *just* to feel sexy again, however, you may be putting too much pressure on yourself. Take it slow, and focus on all the things you like about yourself right now.

Let Me Change into Someone More Comfortable

Can sex and relationships after fifty actually be *better?* Despite all the hardships, some women claim the years following menopause have brought a

ASK YOUR DOCTOR

Prescription Estrogen Products

Oral estrogen therapy usually provides relief from vaginal dryness or thinning. Still, some women who aren't troubled by hot flashes or other symptoms may prefer to treat vaginal thinning locally, by applying estrogen directly to the vaginal tissue. Likewise, some women with severe vaginal symptoms may find these products more effective than oral doses of estrogen, or may, with the supervision of their doctor, use them in addition. Estrogen applied directly to vaginal tissues generally doesn't provide relief from hot flashes; nor does it provide protection against osteoporosis or heart disease.

LIBIDO AND HORMONES

As I mentioned earlier, a loss of drive might be due to any number of physical and lifestyle factors, including vaginal discomfort, stress, fatigue, poor health, and relationship problems. If you've already addressed these issues, however, it's likely there's a hormonal aspect as well.

While estrogen therapy will help restore vaginal tissue, that isn't usually enough to reawaken sexual interest. Numerous studies link a decrease in sex drive to a drop in androgens—specifically testosterone. A study reported in the *Journal of the American Medical Association* compared groups of sexually active and inactive women and found that the sexually active women had naturally higher androgen levels. They also experienced less vaginal atrophy, probably because they stayed sexually active.

Testosterone levels vary greatly in women, and doctors don't know what constitutes a normal amount for any one person. In supplementing testosterone, it's necessary to experiment with doses and preparations. Besides raising sexual interest, testosterone can provide relief from breast tenderness sometimes caused by HRT. Be sure to discuss the testosterone patch (currently awaiting FDA approval), testosterone creams (available through a compounding pharmacy), and Estratest, all of which may help with loss of libido. They are all available from your doctor and require a prescription.

Also, be sure to discuss possible risks with your doctor. Negative side effects can include facial and chest hair, a deeper voice, acne, increased cholesterol, and enlargement of the clitoris.

FOR MEN ONLY—A MENOPAUSE SURVIVAL GUIDE

Did you notice that sometime in the 1980s men stopped saying "My wife's having a baby," in favor of the new phrase: "*We're* having a baby"? I don't suppose men will ever seriously say "*We're* going through menopause"—and yet, why not? As much as menopause is a very personal experience, it's a shared one as well. And so I offer the following six-point survival plan for men who are just realizing that—ready or not—they are about to become menopausal by marriage. As hard as it sometimes is being a perimenopausal woman, I also recognize it's no picnic living with one. I hope this helps!

- **Empathize.** Imagine going through your own midlife crisis under the influence of mood-altering chemicals and you'll have a glimpse of what menopause feels like.
- **Be patient.** Remember that it's simply a natural event, and that the chaotic, out-of-control phase is just temporary.
- **Be understanding.** Accept statements about her feelings without challenge. Realize that what's going on in her head is just as real as what's going on in her body.
- **Be informed.** Remember all the baby books and Lamaze classes when you were getting ready for *that* big event? Doing a little independent research will help allay your fears and make it easier to be supportive. There are even menopause books written *by* men, *for* men. See the Resource List and Suggested Reading section.
- **Offer appropriate support.** I know guys long to fix things, but there's nothing here that's broken. You'll fare better if you leave off the tool belt in favor of a sympathetic ear. What she needs *most* is emotional support and reassurance— these will do more good than any search for a "solution."
- **A little self-sufficiency never hurts.** If you've always depended on her to anticipate and provide for your physical and emotional needs, be prepared to take more responsibility for these yourself. Take on some of the household chores or give her a little break by alternating duties.

Good luck, guys!

sexual rebirth, as exciting in its own way as their younger years. There could be various reasons for this, such as escaping from an unsatisfying marriage to explore new relationships; or it could be the freedom from pregnancy worries and monthly bleeding. But I think there's a deeper reason that has to do with evolving as a person: knowing your body better, feeling a greater sense of self-possession and ability to ask for what you want.

If you *are* fortunate enough to be in a supportive relationship, there's also the greater sense of connection you and your partner can feel from facing life's changes together. After all, any two twenty-year-olds can have a night of wild sex without giving it a thought. But as we get older, the new physical challenges virtually compel us to be more communicative and understanding. The reward is not just good sex, but a deeper, richer bond that can last a lifetime.

Chapter 7

Longevity: Long-Term Health Risks

*The really frightening thing about middle age is
the knowledge that you'll grow out of it.*
—Doris Day

How long is a lifetime? Exactly what ripe old age you will live to may depend on innumerable factors that include everything from how much sleep you get to how safe a driver you are. Still, surveys tell us that, *on average,* a fifty-year-old woman can expect to live to be about eighty-four years old.

Some people are very uncomfortable visualizing their life span. I like the sense of urgency it gives me. I'm fascinated by the finite quality of our lives, and how the simple fact of our mortality affects how we choose to live.

Strange as it sounds, I've gotten into the habit of glancing at the obituaries over breakfast. I find it very motivating. I'll read about someone dying at the age of, say, sixty-two, and I think: "That would mean I'd only have thirteen years left. Wow, that means I *really* have to do something with my life!"

Going by the statistical averages, I have about thirty-five years left. Of course, I want as many of them as possible to be strong, active years. And so, like all women, I have to take into account the *long-term* effects of menopause.

The fact that we may live another one third to one half of our lives at reduced levels of estrogen raises some health concerns. This chapter looks at two major long-term health risks associated with the drop in estrogen—heart disease and bone loss—and describes what you can do to stay healthy over the long run. I'll also describe some of the ongoing research into a new area of concern—cognitive function.

Heart Disease

Heart disease—a man's problem, right? Actually, half of all women over fifty will die from cardiovascular disease, making it the top killer of women and men alike. Because my father succumbed to a heart attack when he was only forty-two years old, I'm very aware of the need to manage my risk. Yet most women, I think, don't realize how widespread that risk really is.

Although nature shields women during our reproductive years, our risk for heart disease begins a sharp upward climb at about age fifty-five, and then continues rising at approximately the same rate as a man's. The risk of heart disease dwarfs that of breast cancer—from which only 4 percent of women will die—and, in fact, outdistances that of all cancers combined. Although there's some comfort in the fact that deaths from heart disease tend to occur later in life than deaths from cancer, heart disease is still the single biggest threat to our long-term health. The good news is that much of that risk can be reduced.

Types of Heart Disease

The terms *heart disease* and *cardiovascular disease* include a number of conditions of the heart and blood vessels. The most common is *coronary artery disease* (also called *coronary heart disease*), which accounts for about half of all deaths from heart disease.

Coronary artery disease is caused by the buildup of fatty substances called *plaque* that accumulate inside vessels around the heart. Plaque narrows the vessels and restricts the flow of blood. It also prevents the walls of the vessels from dilating at times of increased demand, such as during physical exertion or emotional arousal. At such times, inadequate blood flow to the heart may cause chest pain called *angina.* Eventually, a circulating blood clot or spasm of the arterial wall may block the vessel completely, and a heart attack occurs.

Plaque accumulation, or *atherosclerosis,* can also affect blood vessels elsewhere in the body, possibly leading to high blood pressure or stroke.

Estrogen's Protective Effect

Heart disease is neither a symptom nor a direct result of menopause. The risk for heart disease arises after menopause, however, because of the loss of the protective effect of your body's natural estrogen. Researchers believe that estrogen protects premenopausal women by:

- Raising levels of "good" HDL cholesterol while lowering "bad" LDL cholesterol
  - Reducing the rate at which plaque forms
  - Helping vessels dilate, improving flow
  - Possibly reducing clotting

TIP

If you have trouble keeping HDLs and LDLs straight and remembering which are the good guys, here's the key: When it comes to blood lipids, you want to keep your "highs" high, and your "lows" low.

The major detectable change at menopause is a shift in the balance of *HDL* and *LDL.* HDLs, or high-density lipoproteins (often called "good cholesterol"), are responsible for removing cholesterol from the blood, while LDLs, or low-density lipoproteins ("bad cholesterol"), pull more cholesterol into the bloodstream. When it comes to blood lipids, you want keep your "highs" high and your "lows" low. And that's just what estrogen does.

After menopause, though, LDL levels tend to creep up, while HDL levels fall. This creates an unfavorable balance of blood lipids that is one of the major risk factors for heart disease. In the lists that follow are some other factors that increase risk.

Risk Factors for Heart Disease

Biological

- Family history of heart attack, stroke, or coronary bypass before age sixty-five
- African American descent
- Diabetes
- Early menopause, surgical or otherwise
- Postmenopausal
- Blood clots easily
- Tendency to accumulate fat in the upper body (apple shape)
- High blood pressure
- Obesity (more than 30 percent over ideal weight)
- High cholesterol level (over two hundred)
- High triglyceride level (over 250)
- High homocysteine level

Lifestyle

- Smoking
- Physically inactive
- High stress level
- High-fat diet
- More than two alcoholic drinks per day

Lifestyle Changes for a Healthy Heart

What can you do to reduce your risk? Obviously, some factors are out of our control. Although your doctor will take note of family history, race, age, and distribution of fat on your body (all of which are important markers), the key factors in your heart-health profile—the areas you can target through healthier living—are:

- Weight
- Blood pressure
- Total cholesterol level and ratio of HDL and LDL

Most of the beneficial lifestyle changes you can make are aimed at improving these.

Quit Smoking

In the last decade, more than one in five women was a regular smoker, a percentage that's still on the rise among younger women. Smoking raises blood pressure and narrows arteries, increasing your risk for a heart attack (not to mention lung cancer, gum disease, and other serious diseases). What's more, smokers tend to reach menopause up to two years earlier than nonsmokers, which, in turn, raises their risk not only of heart disease but of osteoporosis as well.

According to a recent surgeon general's report, 75 percent of women who smoke say they would like to quit. Yet very few—only about 3 percent—actually do quit each year. For reasons that are not known, women have a harder time quitting than men. Talk with your doctor about nicotine gum, patches, or other methods. As a reward, you'll cut your risk for heart disease in half, so if at first you don't succeed, keep trying.

Eat a Heart-Healthy Diet

When it comes to your bloodstream, you are absolutely what you eat. To help lower blood pressure and improve blood cholesterol, you need a diet generally low in saturated fats and cholesterol. The National Heart, Lung, and Blood Institute suggests that no more than 7 percent of your daily calories come from saturated fat, and that you consume less than 200 milligrams of dietary cholesterol. That means limiting your consumption of foods such as full-fat milk products, fatty meats, tropical oils, partially hydrogenated vegetable oils, and egg yolks. Instead, choose foods high in soluble fiber, such as cereal grains, beans, peas, legumes, and many fruits and vegetables. Select low-fat protein such as lean red meat, skinless chicken, or turkey. When possible, replace red meat with fish or soy protein. (For further nutritional guidelines, see chapter 11.)

Exercise Regularly

Many women who wouldn't think of lighting up a cigarette are still complete slugs when it comes to exercise—yet being sedentary is almost as hard on your heart as smoking! Regular exercise raises HDL levels and, for some people, lowers LDLs as well. A daily thirty-minute dose of moderate-intensity aerobic exercise, such as brisk walking, can cut your heart disease risk almost in half—while at the same time burning calories and improving your mood. See chapters 8 and 9 for more on exercise.

Track Your Cholesterol

Don't you wonder what's going on in your arteries right now? Following new federal guidelines released in 2001, healthy adults should have a full lipoprotein profile every five years to determine their total cholesterol, HDL, LDL, and triclycerides (other fatty substances in the blood). Once you know your numbers, you can start making them go down. According to the National Heart and Lung Association, keeping your overall cholesterol under 200 and your HDL at 60 mg/dL or higher can reduce short-term risk for heart disease by as much as 40 percent, and may lower long-term risk even further.

By the way, just because you're not overweight, don't assume your HDL and LDL numbers are under control. Genetics play a large role in high cholesterol; skinny people can have the problem, too.

Keep Your Weight Down

We've thought for years we needed to keep weight down to look good in our summer fashions, but now there's a much bigger reason. Being more than 20 to 30 percent over your ideal weight is a major strain on the heart. Bringing your weight under control will lower blood pressure and encourage a better balance of HDL and LDL. Don't try for sudden, drastic weight loss—let it be a natural consequence of eating healthier and becoming more physically active.

Track Your Blood Pressure

Even if you've had normal blood pressure all your life, the likelihood of developing high blood pressure increases after menopause. The American Heart Association estimates the nearly two thirds of women over sixty-five have high blood pressure. High blood pressure usually has no symptoms, but it strains the walls of the blood vessels and can lead to heart failure, stroke, and other serious problems. A blood pressure reading of less than 140/90 is considered normal, though many doctors feel optimum values are closer to 120/80. The best prevention and treatment is to keep your weight down, minimize your salt intake, and get checked regularly. If you have hypertension, it's best not to take herbal supplements containing licorice, which can act as a stimulant.

> **ASK YOUR DOCTOR**
>
> Several noninvasive tests can aid early identification of heart problems:
>
> - Electrocardiograms
> - Echocardiography—
>   evaluates heart valves
> - "Fast" CT scans—detect
>   calcium in the coronary arteries

Homocysteine

Homocysteine is an amino acid, the blood level of which has been shown to correlate highly with the risk for heart disease. Blood homocycsteine levels may be lowered by eating foods containing folic acid, such as green leafy vegetables and fruits.

Moderate Alcohol Consumption

People who drink moderate amounts of alcohol have up to 35 percent less heart disease than nondrinkers. However, the key word is *moderation*. For a woman, this means an average of one drink per day. (A drink is 12 ounces of beer, 4 ounces of wine, 1.5 ounces of 80-proof spirits, or 1 ounce of 100-proof spirits.) For women especially, it's a fine line: Moderate alcohol intake raises HDL levels and may reduce blood clotting. However, more than one or two drinks per day raises the risk of breast cancer, high blood pressure, and stroke. Also, in some

> **ASK YOUR DOCTOR**
>
> Many doctors and researchers believe HRT may reduce heart disease risk in healthy women. According to the 2001 report released by the National Heart, Lung, and Blood Institute, however, HRT has *not* been shown to reduce the risk for major coronary events or deaths among postmenopausal women who already *have* heart disease. For them, lifestyle changes and specific cholesterol-lowering drugs may be better choices.

> **SUPPLEMENTS FOR A HEALTHY HEART**
>
> - Folic acid, 800 micrograms a day
> - Vitamin E, 400 to 800 milligrams a day
> - Aspirin, 325 milligrams a day

women, any amount of alcohol may trigger a hot flash. Consult with your doctor before mixing daily aspirin and alcohol consumption.

Bone Loss and Osteoporosis

Although we like to think of our bones as solid and unchanging, they're actually living tissue, in which calcium is constantly being broken down and replenished. Throughout our growing years, we store calcium in our bones faster than we lose it. Sometime in our twenties, though, the tide turns: Bone density starts to level off as the rate of calcium loss catches up with the rate of replenishment.

For a while, the estrogen in our bodies helps make sure that calcium doesn't disappear faster than it's replaced. But as estrogen levels decline, so does calcium replacement. Bone loss begins, slowly at first, but accelerating sharply at menopause to a rate of about 2 percent a year. In some women, it may reach an alarming 3 to 4 percent per year. After about ten years, the rate of loss slows again. Still, a woman may have lost 50 percent or more of her bone density by the time she reaches seventy.

Seventy may seem like a long way off, but the choices you make right now will determine how strong and resilient your skeleton will be in later years. In fact, the *best* time to be thinking about building bone would have been in your twenties, when your net bone mass was still rising. Your thirties and forties are certainly not too early to start taking bone density seriously—fortunately, they're not too late, either.

Men are protected from excessive bone loss by several factors, including a higher initial bone mass, a tendency to be more active, and the effects of testosterone.

Fracture Risk

As bone density decreases, bones become more fragile and prone to fracture—often from very ordinary daily stresses. Up to half of women over fifty in the United States have low bone mass, and 40 percent of U.S. women over fifty will suffer an osteoporotic fracture. The most common types of fracture are those of the wrists and hips, and compression fractures of the vertebrae, which cause loss of height and curvature of the spine.

Hip fractures can be especially devastating, and account for 20 percent of the fractures suffered by the elderly. One in five patients do not survive one year following their surgery (usually due to complications from surgery), and two-thirds never regain the capacity they had before their fall. Having one fracture greatly increases your risk for more falls and more fractures. Bone loss can be the beginning of a downward spiral that is extremely difficult to fight back from.

Fortunately, there have been important advances in treating and preventing osteoporosis in the past thirty years, and there's no reason for our generation to endure the mishaps and misery that previous ones did.

Risk Factors for Osteoporosis

Biological
- Small, thin, frame
- Caucasian or Asian descent
- Family member with osteoporosis
- Premature or induced menopause
- Going six months without a period during reproductive years (not counting pregnancies)
- Never having been pregnant
- Postmenopausal

Long-Term Use Of
- Corticosteroids (such as prednisone or cortisone)
- Anticonvulsants
- Antacids containing aluminum
- Larger than usual doses of thyroid medication

Lifestyle
- Physically inactive
- Smoking
- High consumption of beverages containing caffeine
- High consumption of carbonated beverages containing phosphorus

- High-protein diet
- More than two alcoholic drinks per day
- Low dietary calcium intake
- Lack of sufficient vitamin D

Checking Bone Density

A fracture is, all too often, the first sign of a problem. But it shouldn't be. Although standard X rays are poor at spotting bone loss, effective testing is available. The best is probably the Dual Energy X-Ray Absorptiometry (DEXA) scan, which checks your hip, forearm, and spine. Less expensive, though less comprehensive screenings are also available, such as a heel DEXA or wrist DEXA. Bone density can vary within the body, but these limited scans can provide a good general sense of how your bones are doing.

If you're premenopausal and don't have significant risk factors for osteoporosis, most experts agree that testing is not essential. Once you do reach menopause, they recommend a DEXA scan to establish a baseline to help you evaluate changes in later life. Other doctors, however, feel that a single baseline screening should be done well before menopause, to ensure the optimum bone density maintenance.

You should be tested now if:

- You are past menopause and are not taking HRT.
- You are over sixty and have never taken HRT.
- You have lost two inches in height.
- Regular X rays have indicated low bone density.
- You have any chronic diseases or have been using medications associated with bone loss.
- You have had a fracture.

Lifestyle Measures to Prevent Osteoporosis

While estrogen therapy is the most effective treatment for osteoporosis, it can only slow the rate of loss, not build new bone. That's why even if you decide to take HRT at some time in the future, it's important not to wait for a problem to occur, but to undertake lifestyle measures *right now* to hang on to the bone you still have.

Many of the lifestyle habits that benefit your heart can reduce your rate of bone loss and your risk of osteoporosis as well. Not smoking, limiting your alcohol intake, and eating a balanced diet are all important for maintaining healthy bones. In addition, there are several other important steps you can take, targeted especially at fortifying your skeleton.

Weight-Bearing Exercise

Recent research has shown that weight training and other forms of load-bearing exercise play an important role in keeping your bones strong. Your bones naturally adapt to stresses placed on them by exercise. Even a brief weight training routine involving just one exercise for each major muscle group, done two or three times a week, can substantially strengthen your bones. Other forms of exercise such as jogging, stair climbing, and brisk walking also work well.

Load-bearing exercise builds not only bone but also strength and balance, thereby reducing risk of fracture. See chapter 8 for more about weight training for healthy bones.

Dietary Calcium

The prime time to be getting adequate calcium in your diet is before age twenty, while your bones are still forming. Dietary calcium is still one of the most important things you can give your bones, however. Studies have shown that getting adequate calcium can increase spinal bone mineral density (BMD) and reduce fractures. The more calcium you can get from food, the better, but it's a good idea to take a calcium supplement as well. The National Academy of Science recommends:

Before age 50	1,000 mg
Age 50–65 (with HRT)	1,000 mg
Age 50–65 (no HRT)	1,500 mg
Over age 65	1,500 mg

In addition, it's important to steer clear of foods that can rob your body of calcium. Large amounts of protein, salt, caffeine, or phosphorus (from carbonated beverages) can all increase the rate at which calcium is lost in the urine.

Calcium carbonate pills (such as Tums) are an inexpensive source of calcium. For those who have trouble digesting calcium carbonate, calcium citrate is better absorbed and may have fewer gastrointestinal side effects.

Vitamin D

Vitamin D is necessary for absorption of calcium. Our bodies naturally manufacture vitamin D when our skin is exposed to sunlight. Exercising outdoors can be a good source of vitamin D, although prolonged sun exposure damages the skin and increases the risk of skin cancer. That's why it's important to supplement your sun exposure by consuming milk and other vitamin-D-enriched products, along with taking 400 to 800 IU of vitamin D daily in pill form. Many calcium supplements also contain vitamin D.

> **ASK YOUR DOCTOR**
>
> Doctors contend that taking estrogen replacement therapy for five to ten years will reduce your fracture risk by half. The question is whether it's better to take estrogen in your fifties when bone mass is still relatively high, or to wait until your sixties and seventies, when the risk of fracture is higher.

Soy

Keep eating that tofu! Research suggests that estrogenic effects of the isoflavones in soy may help protect your bones. In a recent study at the University of Illinois, postmenopausal women who took 40 grams of soy protein powder per day (containing 90 milligrams of isoflavones) increased their spinal bone density, while significantly improving blood cholesterol levels as well.

By staying active and eating well—as well as exploring your medical options with your doctor—you can limit the long-term risks of these diseases and ensure yourself the best possible shot at a long, healthy life.

ASK YOUR DOCTOR

Various drugs, some relatively new, are currently being prescribed for post-menopausal women with low bone density:

- Fossamax.
- Evista.
- Miacalcin (calcitonin).
- Slow-release fluoride.
- Raloxifene, a SERM (selective estrogen receptor modulator) "designer estrogen" designed to minimize the cancer risks from standard estrogen therapy, has been shown to reduce risk of vertebral fracture by 36 percent.
- Tamoxifen is used to treat or prevent breast cancer and has been shown to have a positive effect on bone mass, but there is no data yet on whether it prevents fracture.

Some of these drugs have potentially dangerous side effects—be sure your doctor explains the risks and benefits of any therapeutic approach you're considering.

Visualization Exercise

YOUR FUTURE IS IN YOUR HANDS

"Live every day as if it were your last!" That sounds like good advice, but realistically, it doesn't make sense to stop exercising or paying your bills. On the other hand, I don't try to pretend I'm going to live forever, because I wouldn't feel motivated to accomplish anything. Here's an exercise designed to give you a realistic perspective of your place in life, based on the average life expectancy of a fifty-year-old woman.

Go to that jar or drawer where you keep all your change, and count out eighty-four pennies. Holding them in one hand, take away a penny for every year you've lived. Hold *those* pennies in the other hand.

Now compare hands: In one palm, your life already lived; in the other, the remainder—your life to come. How do the two piles stack up? How does it feel to see them? Is it very different from how you imagined it?

Now look at the pennies that represent your future. Whatever their number, they're yours to spend. What sort of life will you use them to buy?

A NEW AREA OF RESEARCH: HORMONES AND THE BRAIN

Women are two to three times as likely as men to develop Alzheimer's disease. This happens in part because women outlive men, but some researchers now think it's related to estrogen loss as well. Dementia affects 10 percent of women over the age of sixty-five, and 50 percent of women over eighty-five.

According to Daniel Cosgrove, M.D., of the WellMax Center in La Quinta, CA, several independent lines of evidence support the idea that low levels of estrogen are not good for the brain.

• Estrogen *nurtures* brain cells, and the lack of it leads to decreased function in the laboratory. Estrogen also has an antioxidant function that protects neurons from free radicals. Laboratory research demonstrates that brain cells have estrogen receptors, and that *human* estrogen (but not phytoestrogens) attaches to these receptors.

• Estrogen *use* is associated with better brain function. Several studies comparing nondemented active women found that estrogen users had higher scores on various brain function tests than nonusers.

• Low *blood levels* of estrogen correlate with impaired brain function. One study found that women with Alzheimer's were four to six times more likely to have low estradiol levels (under 20 pg/ml) than normal controls. Other studies found that when comparing active, nondemented women of the same age, those with higher estrogen blood levels performed better on brain function tests. (Blood levels vary greatly among individuals, even among those not taking replacement doses.)

Armed with this evidence, researchers recently investigated whether estrogen could be used to treat Alzheimer's and reverse dementia, but these efforts were not successful. However, more research is being done to clarify estrogen's role in *preventing* or delaying cognitive decline. Meanwhile, some of the best things you can do to retain mental capacity are to stay active, both mentally and physically, and take supplemental antioxidants (especially vitamin E).

Chapter 8
Strength Training

I think these difficult times have helped me to understand better than before how infinitely rich and beautiful life is in every way and that so many things that one goes around worrying about are of no importance whatsoever.
—Isak Dineson

As I get older, I realize that each season of life has its own beauty. As much as I still appreciate the freshness and vitality of a twenty-year-old, the beauty of midlife is richer and more varied. What makes a woman beautiful at fifty is her depth and character, her conversation and spirit—it's a whole package.

And when it comes to our bodies, well, let's just say standards change a little. What's important now isn't cosmetic perfection, it's how well our bodies work and what they say about us, through qualities like posture and energy.

When I race downhill on skis or charge up one of my favorite mountain trails, I feel free—like a cheetah or a gazelle. In those moments, time stands still. It's a wonderful feeling, and I've found the best way to hang on to it through the years is to stay *strong*.

Of all the healthy lifestyle habits you could adopt at midlife, resistance training, or strength training, is perhaps the most important. Of course, I don't mean you should give up aerobic exercise or healthy eating habits. But only strength training offers these vital benefits:

- Burns more total calories than aerobic exercise, by raising your metabolism
- Fortifies your bones to help prevent osteoporosis and bone fractures
- Improves posture for spinal health and confidence
- Improves poise and balance to avoid falls and injury

Postmenopausal women get an extra benefit from their lean muscle, too. Because muscle tissue is able to convert testosterone into estrone, a form of estrogen, building lean muscle through regular exercise can increase estrogen production after menopause.

Burning Fat at Fifty—The Secret Is Muscle

The other night, I found a frantic message from a friend on my answering machine: "Kathy, I'm desperate . . . [dramatic pause] . . . It's my thighs." (Yes, I really get messages like this.) "I don't know what's going on— they're exploding! The fat is *flooding* everywhere! There's no shape, there's no tone; I can't stand them anymore!" With a heavy sigh, she said, "It must be menopause."

Why do so many women seem to gain weight at menopause? *Is* it hormonal? Some researchers have theorized that, because fat tissue produces small amounts of estrogen, the body stocks up on fat to compensate for the decline in estrogen production from the ovaries. Still, there's no evidence that a decrease in estrogen *causes* weight gain.

The main reason we gain weight is that menopause occurs at a time when we just happen to be turning fifty. By that age, we've had about two decades during which we've been losing our skeletal muscle mass. This happens due to genetic factors, as well as decreasing activity levels. Without adequate muscle, our metabolism plummets, and it's much harder to burn calories.

My desperate friend is an avid walker—practically religious about it. But aerobic exercise by itself isn't enough anymore. Here's why.

The Real Secret to Burning Calories

First, forget about exercise burning calories. What really burns calories is *muscle.* Having more muscle gives you the power to burn more calories than you could without it. It's that simple.

Muscle burns calories three ways:

- While working out—more muscle gives you the strength and stamina to work with greater intensity.
- After working out—training at a higher intensity raises your metabolism, and causes it to stay high for several hours afterward. That metabolic bump will cause your body to burn more calories *between* workouts than you would otherwise.
- Around the clock—Your muscle tissue is like a furnace, burning more calories *all the time.*

So if you want to lose excess weight, stop focusing only on the calories you burn *during* exercise, and start working to increase your body's overall calorie-burning potential, by increasing your muscle mass.

Build Your Bones to Go the Distance

I'm not saying this to scare you—well, maybe just a little—but the National Osteoporosis Foundation estimates that up to half the women in this country over fifty have low bone mass, and that 40 percent will eventually fracture a bone as a result. These fractures—particularly hip fractures—can be debilitating and even life threatening.

The good news is that strength training can prevent or reverse bone loss at a rate of as much as 1 percent a year or more. In a study reported in the *Journal of Applied Physiology* (May 1998), researchers observed increases in bone mineral density in subjects who exercised that were comparable to—and actually slightly *greater* than—those obtained using HRT! (Gains were even greater in subjects who exercised and took estrogen too.)

ASK YOUR DOCTOR
WEIGHT GAIN FROM HRT
Weight gain is one of the biggest reasons women don't continue with HRT. Typically, this is caused by bloating and can sometimes be eliminated by adjusting your medication.

The bone-strengthening benefits of weight training are one of the best examples of how exercise improves your quality of life. Even if you didn't add a day to your actual life span, strength training can increase the number of high-quality years you enjoy by a decade or more.

Because the most common fractures are those of the wrists, hips, and vertebrae, our strength training program will give special attention to these areas. Plus, it will include exercises for all major muscle groups to tone and tighten your whole body.

Your Posture: Don't Let Gravity Decide

I get a lot of compliments on my posture, and it makes me realize what a strong impression posture makes. When you stand and sit with good posture, you're less likely to injure yourself in daily activity. Your internal organs have room to breathe. You radiate confidence and command respect. Your clothes fit better, and you get through the day with less fatigue.

Best of all, improving your posture makes you instantly look *slimmer.*

You only have to look around you to see the effect that aging can have on our bodies. I'm always shocked by the appearance of people who, after years of bone loss and poor posture, seem to stand in a permanent cringe. That's why I urge you to start putting effort into your posture *now.* It takes only a few minutes a week. Don't let gravity have the last word!

The full-body routine that follows contains a number of exercises to help you build core strength for better posture. Be sure to check with your doctor before beginning this or any strength training program.

Posture

1. Good Standing Posture
2. Midback Strengthener with Wall Guide

Leg and Buttocks Strength

1. L-Sit with Wall Guide
2. Wall Sit
3. Balance Knee Extension
4. Squat
    Variation: Squat with Abduction (Side Lifts)
    Variation: Squat with Lean/Overload
5. Step-Back Lunges
    Variation: Front Lunges
6. Rear Leg Lift (Ankle Weights Optional)
7. Toe Raises on Stair (Balance Option on Floor)

Leg and Buttocks Core Strength

1. Face-Up Plank with Leg Pull
2. Face-Down Plank with Leg Pull
3. Bridge

Back and Buttocks Core Strength

1. Dead Lift
2. Double Leg Kick
3. Cross Crawl
4. Superman

Arm and Shoulder Strength

1. Front Raise/Rear Raise
2. Side Lateral Raise with Retraction
3. Biceps Curls
4. Plank Forearm Hover
5. Triceps Kickback with Hip Hinge
6. One-Arm Double-Bell Row
7. Back Flye
8. Military Press (Overhead Press)
9. Push-Ups (Three Levels)

Abdominal Core Strength

1. House for a Mouse
2. Tabletop Alternating Legs*
3. Leg Slides*
4. Alternating Leg Lifts*
5. One Hundred
6. Obliques Using Lateral Flexion
7. Boat (with Assisted Lift into Intensity with Arms)

*No spinal flexion—these are good options for those who know they have osteoporosis in their spine.

Choice of Exercises

The choice of exercises for your routine is up to you. Using the exercises in this chapter, you can put together any combination you like. To help you get a balanced workout, I've grouped them in categories by body part. I recommend starting with a routine of ten to fifteen exercises, including several examples from each category, and then adding or substituting other exercises over time.

For Best Results, Keep a Training Diary

I suggest keeping a diary of your routine, consisting of a list of exercise names and a record of how many sets, reps, and—when applicable—how much weight you lifted. This will not only make it easier to remember your routine, but it will also help you track your progress.

How to Progress

For the exercises involving bodyweight:

I've provided tips in many of the descriptions for making the exercise harder through variations in body position. Following these guidelines, you'll be able to progress to higher levels as you get stronger.

For the exercises involving free weights:

Always choose an amount of weight that will allow you to reach fatigue within the prescribed rep range, usually 8–12 repetitions. Use progressively heavier weights as your strength improves, but only use as much as you can lift with correct form.

Note to beginners:

If you're new to weight training, *start very slow and easy:* Where weights are called for, use very light ones and progress gradually. At first, focus on technique more than on fatiguing the muscles. Study the exercise instructions carefully, and try to develop a feel for the muscle being trained in each case.

Kathy's Sample Routine

EXERCISE	REPETITIONS	NOTES
Squats	12–15 reps	Start with 3–5 pound dumbbells, then increase to 8 pounds.
Squats (w/Side Lift)	12 reps each leg	When it gets too easy, add 1- to 3-pound ankle weights.
Rear Leg Lift	12 reps each leg	When it gets too easy, add 1- to 3-pound ankle weights.
Toe Raises on Stair	12–15 reps	When you're ready for more resistance, do one leg at a time.
Dead Lifts	Work up to 12 reps	First, work on perfect form using no weight. Eventually, begin using 5–10 pound weights and add more as you get stronger.
Side Lateral Raise w/Retraction	12–15 reps	Start with 3–5 pound weights and increase when you can do 12–15 reps comfortably.
Biceps Curls	12–15 reps	Start with 5–8 pound weights.
Triceps Kickback w/Hip Hinge	12–15 reps	Start with 3–5 pound weights.
One-Arm Double-Bell Row	12–15 reps	Start with 5–8 pound weights.
Back Flye	12–15 reps	Start with 3–5 pound weights.
Push-Ups	12–15 reps	At first, support yourself on your knees. Eventually, try lowering yourself with your weight on your toes, and pushing back up on your knees.
Tabletop Alternating Legs	Start with 12 reps/leg	To increase intensity, move legs farther from your center (away from a tuck) and straighten knees slightly.
Obliques w/Lateral Flexion	Start with 12 reps/side	
Cross Crawl	Start with 12 reps/side	
Double Leg Kick	Start with 6 reps/side	

Guidelines for Performing Each Exercise

• Perform reps slowly and with control, approximately four to seven seconds per rep, unless otherwise noted.

• Keep rest periods between sets and exercise to forty-five seconds or less.

• Try to reach fatigue within the prescribed rep range, maintaining proper form throughout.

• Focus! Perform every rep with concentration and commitment.

Scheduling

• Do at least two workouts per week. You can either do a full-body routine (involving exercises from all body part categories), or split it in half and do two mini-workouts at different times.

• Rest forty-eight hours between workouts for the same body parts.

As a beginner, start by doing one set of each exercise, using the rep ranges shown. After your body adjusts to the training, you'll progress faster if you start adding more weight. Your goal should be to use enough weight that your muscles fatigue in about 8–12 reps. Once you can reach 12 reps again, it is time to increase the weight. Another way to increase the intensity and boost results is to do two sets per exercise. Keep rests between sets to about forty-five seconds or less.

Good Standing Posture

Targets: How to stand tall and straight, keeping your pelvis in a neutral position.

Setup: Stand with your feet hip distance apart, and your weight evenly distributed on your feet. Don't let your feet turn outward.

1. Legs are straight. (Knees should not be hyperextended or locked. To keep from hyperextending, make your quadriceps active by tightening the quadriceps muscles; you should see your kneecap lifting up toward your hip.)
2. Pelvis is in a neutral position. The pubic bone and the anterior superior iliac spine (ASIS) should be in the same vertical plane.
3. The belly is drawn in toward the spine (transverse abdominis pulled in). This is *not* the diaphragm; you should still be able to take a full breath.
4. Rib cage is funneled down toward the top of the pelvis.
5. Breast bone (sternum) is lifted.
6. Collar bones (clavicles) are wide, long, and open.
7. Shoulder blades (scapulae) are pulled down toward your waist.
8. Shoulders are pressed down, creating lots of space between them and your ears.
9. Neck is elongated and throat is relaxed.
10. Chin is parallel to the floor.
11. Ears, shoulders, and hips should be the same level right and left.

Comments: Practice doing all these cues at once. This is a workout in itself! As you get familiar with these postural cues, you will be better able to incorporate perfect posture into your workout exercises. Remember, practice does not make perfect. Only perfect practice makes perfect!

Midback Strengthener with Wall Guide

Targets: Upper back postural strength and flexibility of the front of the shoulder.

Setup: Stand with your back to a wall, touching heels, buttocks, upper back, and head. Bend your elbows 90 degrees and lift them to your sides at shoulder height. Press your elbows and hands against the wall. If you have tight shoulders, you may not be able to touch the wall with your hands, elbows, or both—focus on your effort.

Move: Widen your clavicles, funnel your ribs down toward your waist, and press your navel toward your spine. Keeping your elbows and hands against the wall, if possible, slide your arms overhead. Continuing to maintain pressure and effort, slide back down to shoulder level. Repeat six to eight times.

Focus: Maintain a neutral spine (your low back is not pressing against the wall, but your abdominals are engaged, pulling your navel toward your spine).

Comments: The effort in the postural muscles in your upper back will help stretch the front of your shoulders, enabling you to have the flexibility and strength to maintain or improve your posture.

L-Sit with Wall Guide

Targets: Thighs (quadriceps femoris), hip flexors, abdominals, and postural muscles.

Setup: Sit against a wall, with your legs straight in front of you. Now move ½ inch away from the wall. Bend your right knee. If you feel your back touching the wall, it means your spine is flexed; lift your spine back up to neutral so it doesn't touch the wall.

Move: Tighten your left thigh and try to lift it off the floor—enough space between the floor and your leg to slip a piece of paper underneath is fine. If doing so causes your back or head to touch the wall, your spine moved again and you need to straighten up.

Focus: Use your abdominals and postural muscles to keep your body straight while lifting your leg. This exercise is as much about maintaining good posture as it is about strengthening your thighs.

Comments: Start by doing six to eight lifts with each leg. As you get stronger, you can try holding a single lift for thirty to sixty seconds per leg.

Wall Sit

Targets: Thighs (quadriceps femoris), hip flexors, abdominals, and postural muscles.

Setup: Standing against a wall, move your feet away from the wall so that when you slide down to a 90-degree angle of the hips and knees, you will also have your ankle–knee line perpendicular to the floor.

Move: For beginners, holding this move is enough. When you're ready to add difficulty, try lifting one leg and straightening that knee. Hold the leg out there for five to ten seconds. Repeat on the other side. Work up to six to eight repetitions on each leg.

Focus: Keep your spine in neutral, abdominals pressed in, shoulder blades pressed toward your waist, clavicles wide, neck elongated.

Comments: To build up one leg at a time, start by just lifting your heel; feel the overload as you shift your weight off of that leg. Or try doing the exercise a little higher on the wall with one leg, gradually moving back down to the lower level.

Balance Knee Extension

Targets: Thighs (quadriceps femoris), hip flexors, abdominals, and postural muscles.

Setup: Standing balanced on one leg, lift your other leg so your knee is as high as your hip.

Move: Trying to keep your knee at hip height, straighten your knee until you can squeeze the thigh muscle (your knee might drop from hip height—especially after a rep or two).

Focus: The speed of this exercise should be very slow. Try to hold the straight knee for a count of five or longer. Do six to eight repetitions on each leg.

Comments: As you straighten your knee, focus on maintaining your posture. Your spine may flex or slouch, and it's possible that you may try leaning back to counterbalance the weight of your leg as it straightens. The goal is to stimulate the abdominals and postural muscles while completing the exercise. You may want to be near a wall or chair to check your balance.

Squat

Targets: Thighs and buttocks (quadriceps, hamstrings, and gluteals).

Setup: Feet hip width apart, abdominals tight, chest open.

Move: Inhale, and lower your hips until your thighs are nearly parallel to the floor. Your spine should be as straight as it was when you were standing. Exhale as you return to standing.

Focus: Tailbone reaches back, spine stays in neutral (be careful that your back does not round). Your knees stay as close to over your ankle as possible—make sure they don't shoot past your toes.

Comments: Once you can do a perfect-form set of eight to twelve squats, add weight using your dumbbells or a barbell.

Variation: Squat with Abduction (Side Lifts)

As you rise out of the squat, lift your right leg, keeping your foot parallel to the other. Repeat the squat with the lift. Do eight to twelve repetitions on one leg, then repeat on the other leg.

Variation: Squat with Lean/Overload

Go down into your squat, then shift your weight onto your right leg, leaning and overloading that leg. Make sure your hip doesn't jut out, and that your knees don't buckle in or out. Return to center position, then rise. Do about eight to twelve repetitions on each leg.

Comments: The Squat with Lean/Overload is a great option to work the legs with more intensity if the dumbbells you have are not heavy enough to get the quads tired in those eight to twelve repetitions.

Step-Back Lunges

Targets: Buttocks (gluteals), front and back of thigh (quadriceps and hamstrings).

Setup: Stand straight with your feet hip width apart, abdominals pulled up and in, upper body posture open and erect, and dumbbells held by your side.

Move: Inhale, and take a large step back with your right leg. Go back far enough so that as you dip down, bending both knees, your front knee stays over your front ankle. Your back knee should be under your hip. The front thigh will be almost parallel to the ground. Your back heel will be lifted. Exhale and push off, returning to standing.

Focus: Try to keep more of your body weight on the front leg. As you get stronger, try to use your front leg to more slowly lower yourself down into the lunge, and more slowly raise your body weight out of the lunge to home position. Do eight to twelve repetitions.

Comments: If you have trouble with balance, practice the movement without weights with a chair nearby so you can check your balance.

Variation: Front Lunges:
A Front Lunge is similar in execution, except that your right foot steps forward and returns to home position. Make sure you step out far enough that your front knee doesn't jut out farther than your toe (you want your front ankle directly under your front knee).

Rear Leg Lift (Ankle Weights Optional)

Targets: Buttocks (gluteals) and back of the thigh (hamstrings).

Setup: Stand a foot or so away from a chair. Hinge forward at the hips (the spine does not flex). Move your right leg slightly behind your left so that your right toes are on the floor near your left heel. Your right heel is off the ground.

Move: Slowly lift your right leg as high as you can without arching your back as you exhale. Pause, inhale, and lower it back down. Do eight to twelve repetitions on each leg.

Focus: Keep your upper body posture perfect while you perform this exercise. Your working hip should not be higher than your standing-leg hip—your hips should be level.

Comments: Ankle weights should be added once you can perform the repetitions with ease.

Variations: Perform the exercise with your foot coming straight off the ground, or turned out from the hip (like ballet's first position) to challenge the lateral part of the hamstrings and glutes, or turned in from the hip (pigeon toed) to challenge the medial part of the hamstrings and glutes and inner thigh.

Toe Raises on Stair (Balance Option on Floor)

Targets: Calf muscles (gastrocnemius, soleus).

Setup: Standing on a stair or similar platform, balance on the ball of one foot, with your heel hanging off the edge of the stair.

Move: Inhale, and slowly lower your heel until you feel a gentle stretch in your calf muscles. Exhale, and push up onto the ball of your foot, lifting your heel as high as you can. Pause at the top, inhale, and lower back down. Do eight to twelve repetitions on each leg.

Focus: Remember to keep your postural muscles active, abs pulled in, and shoulders down away from your ears.

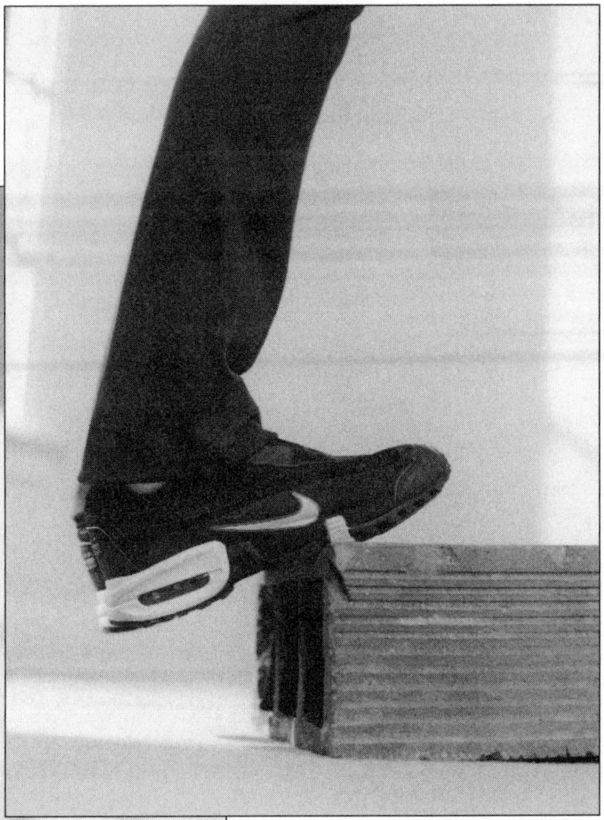

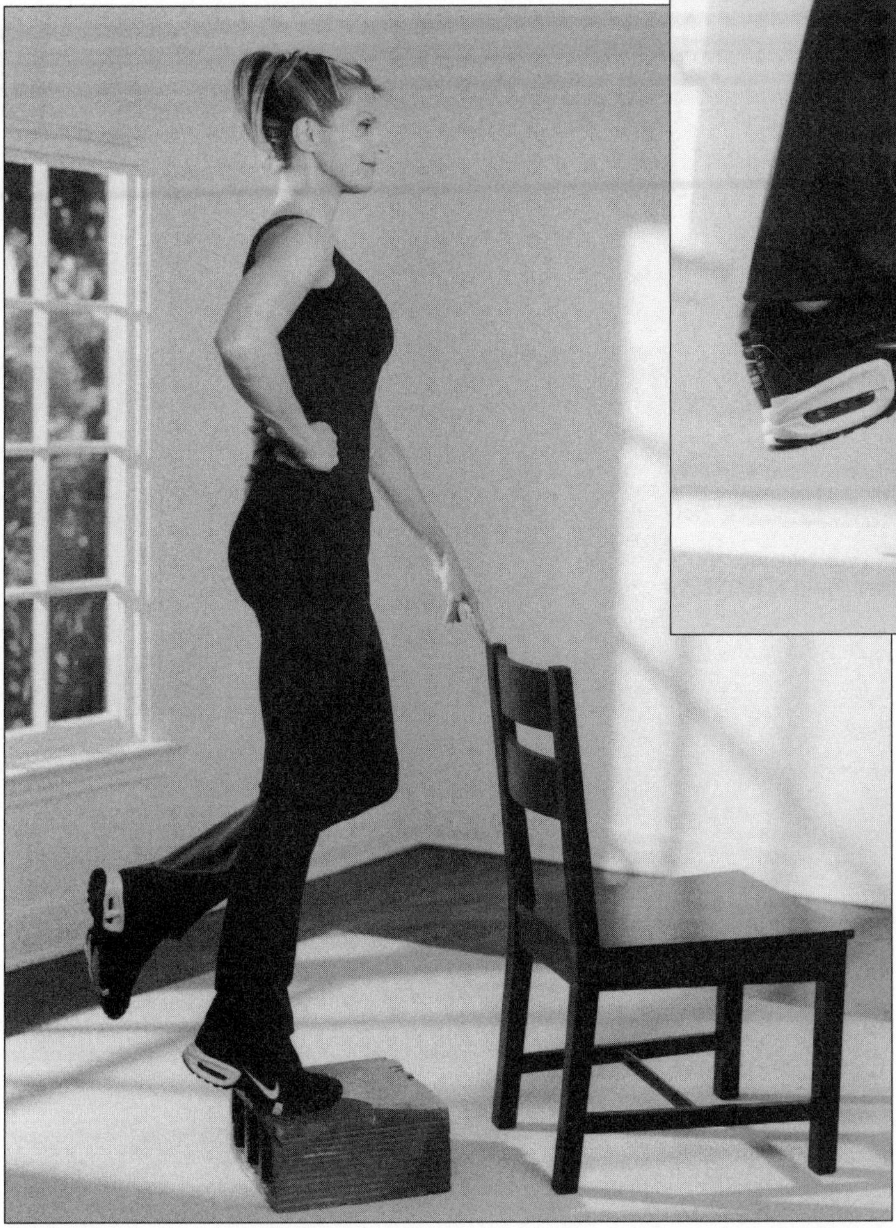

Face-Up Plank with Leg Pull

Targets: Shoulders, buttocks, hamstrings, low back.

Setup: Begin seated on the floor with your legs extended straight. Place your hands near your buttocks with fingers either facing your rear, or out to the side.

Move: Lift your hips off the floor into a bridge, keeping your collarbones wide, your shoulder blades depressed, your abdominals pulled in, and your neck lengthened.

Focus: Breathe deeply and try and hold this position for up to half a minute.

Comments: If it bothers you to be on your hands, try holding a dumbbell and curling your fingers under to get your wrist into a neutral position.

Variation: After you lift your plank into a high bridge, keep your hips high and shift your weight to one leg. If you can, lift the other leg off the floor. Alternate right and left sides and work up to four to eight sets.

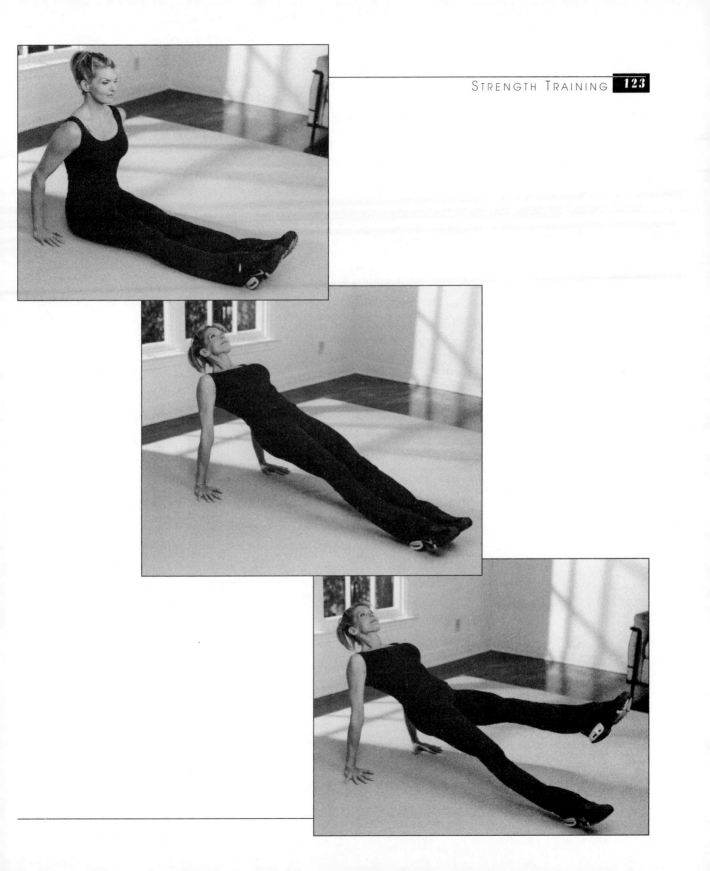

Face-Down Plank with Leg Pull

Targets: Shoulders, abdominals, legs, and hips.

Setup: From a kneeling position, move out to a military push-up position with your weight evenly distributed between your feet and your hands. Pull your abdominals up hard. Squeeze your buttocks muscles for additional core stabilization.

Move: Shift your weight onto your right leg, and, if you can, lift your left leg off the floor, maintaining the straight body. Repeat shifting your weight and trying to lift your right leg. Do four to eight sets.

Focus: Remember to work your postural muscles of the shoulder; also, widen your collarbones, press your shoulder blades toward your waist, and lengthen your neck.

Comments: If your abdominals and buttocks (core) muscles don't work hard in this exercise, your buttocks may sag down, creating compression in the low back. It's very important that you use those core muscles to prevent your middle from sagging, and—as you fatigue—to remain aware of this and stop to rest when your form begins to deteriorate.

Bridge

Targets: Buttocks (gluteals) and back of thigh (hamstrings).

Setup: Lie on your back with your knees bent and feet close together. Starting with your tailbone, peel your spine off the floor, vertebra by vertebra, until you're as high as your mid–shoulder blade. Squeeze your inner thighs together.

Move: Drop your hips and drive them back up to a high bridge, keeping your inner thighs squeezed together.

Focus: Feel your gluteal muscles squeeze together in the bridge, and your inner thighs—knee to pelvis—pressed tight together.

Comments: When you can do eight to twelve reps comfortably, lift your right leg off the floor and do the exercise with just your left leg on the floor. Then repeat, taking your left leg off the floor.

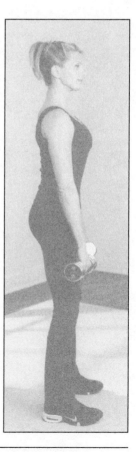

Dead Lift

Targets: Low back (erector spinae, quadratus lumborum), buttocks (gluteals), and hamstrings.

Setup: Standing upright with your feet shoulder width apart, your knees almost straight, and holding a fairly heavy weight.

Move: Hinging at the hips (there is no spinal flexion here—your back does not round), lower the weights down to your knee area, pressing your hips and tailbone back. Keep your shoulder blades down toward your waist, your collarbones wide, your neck long, your abdominals pulled up and in. Return to standing.

Focus: If you have tight hamstrings, you may find you cannot go down as low as your knees. If you go too far, your back will start to round.

Comments: If you need more intensity, but don't have access to heavy enough weights, try this one-legged option. Use the same cues from above, but put your left leg behind the right one. Keep very little weight on your left leg, almost balancing on your right. Do the Dead Lift for the right leg in this manner. Do eight to twelve repetitions, then repeat the exercise with your left leg in front.

Double Leg Kick

Targets: Transverse abdominis, low back muscles, gluteals, and hamstrings.

Setup: Lie prone with your knees bent, looking to the right, hands clasped on your low back, transverse abdominis engaged lifting your navel toward your spine (making a "house for a mouse"—see Abdominal Core Strength).

Move: Kick your heels toward your buttocks three times. As you straighten your knees, lift your upper body, depressing and retracting your shoulder blades, lengthening your neck, and keeping the "house for the mouse." Lower yourself back to the start position, looking left. Repeat five sets (alternating by starting the exercise looking right, then looking left).

Focus: Focus on your upper body posture as you lift and straighten your legs.

Comments: If you really work the "house for the mouse," you won't go as high in the lift phase of the exercise.

Cross Crawl

Targets: Low back (erector spinae, quadratus lumborum), buttocks (gluteals), and hamstrings.

Setup: Lie prone, your neck in neutral position. Pull your naval toward your spine (making a "house for a mouse"—see Abdominal Core Strength).

Move: Lift your right arm with your left leg. Repeat with the left arm/right leg. Do eight to twelve sets.

Focus: Focus on lengthening rather than lifting high. Try to keep your navel lifted off the floor.

Comments: If the exercise is too difficult, modify it by having your arms closer to your shoulders, rather than stretched out. You could also break it into two exercises by lifting your arms and shoulders only—keeping your feet and legs on the floor—then doing the second set by keeping your arms and shoulders on the floor, lifting just your legs.

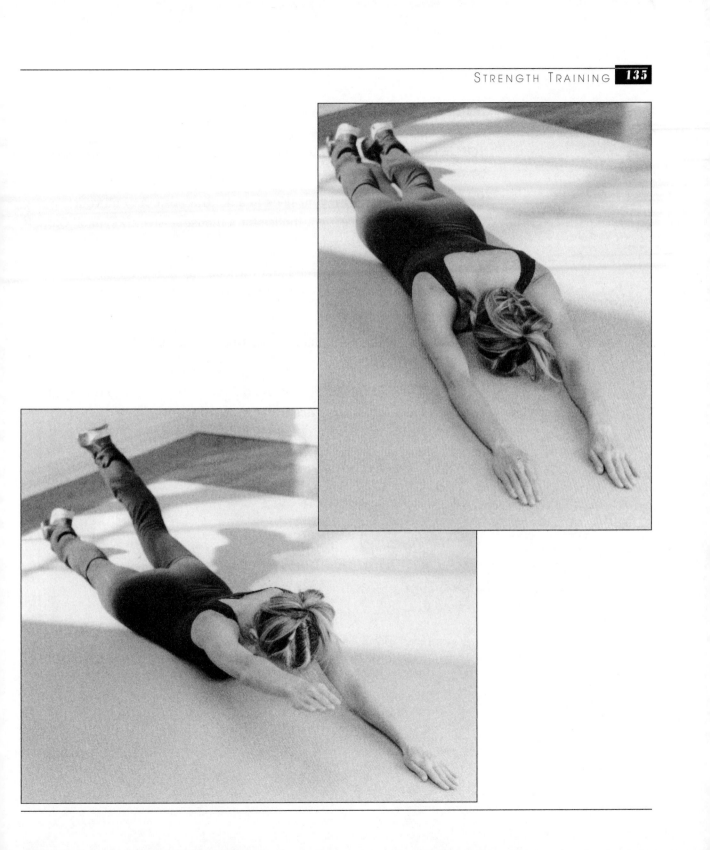

Superman

Targets: Low back (erector spinae, quadratus lumborum), buttocks (gluteals), and hamstrings.

Setup: Lie prone, with your neck in a neutral position. Pull your navel toward your spine (making a "house for a mouse"—see Abdominal Core Strength).

Move: With your arms stretched overhead, lift your arms/shoulders and feet/legs. Hold for a count of five, then release down. Do eight to twelve repetitions.

Focus: Focus on lengthening rather than lifting high. Try to keep your navel lifted off the floor.

Comments: If the exercise is too difficult, you could also break it into two exercise by lifting your arms and shoulders only—keeping your feet and legs on the floor—then doing the second set by keeping your arms and shoulders on the floor, lifting just your legs.

Front Raise/Rear Raise

Targets: Shoulders (anterior and posterior deltoids).

Setup: Stand with your feet hip width apart, knees slightly bent, collarbones widened, shoulder blades pressed down, shoulders away from your ears, abdominals pulled up and in, and neck lengthened. Holding a dumbbell in each hand by your side, turn your palms so they're facing each other.

Move: For a front raise, lift the weights to shoulder height as you exhale. For a rear raise, lift the weights behind you as high as you can go as you exhale. Pause, inhale, and lower the weight.

Focus: Keep your shoulders in perfect posture as you execute the movements.

Comments: Do eight to twelve front raises, and eight to twelve rear raises.

Side Lateral Raise with Retraction

Targets: Medial and posterior deltoids (your shoulder muscles), and rhomboids (muscles around your scapula).

Setup: Hold your weights with your palms facing your sides (a modified position is palms facing up), feet shoulder width apart, body erect, abdominals and postural muscles engaged, and neck lengthened.

Move: Slow and controlled, lift the weights to shoulder height. Squeeze your shoulder blades together as if you have a pencil on your spine that you're trying to hold there (that movement of the shoulder blades is called retraction)—and at the same time, try to keep your shoulder blades pressed down toward your waist. Now lower the weights back to your sides, keeping your shoulder blades engaged.

Focus: The weight should never swing with momentum. The lifting and the lowering of the weight should be deliberate and controlled.

Comments: Think of your arms as ending at your shoulder blades, not your shoulders, trying to keep the shoulder blades depressed—pressed toward your waist. Watch that your shoulders don't elevate—come toward your ears. Keep as much space as you can between your shoulders and your ears.

Biceps Curls

Targets: Front of your upper arms (biceps).

Setup: Stand straight with your feet hip width apart. Pull your abdominals up and in, widen your collarbones, depress your shoulder blades, press your shoulders down away from your ears, and lengthen your neck. Have your knees straight but not locked, with your weight evenly distributed between your toes and your heels. Hold a dumbbell in each hand, palms facing your body, with your elbows straight but not locked. Your elbows should stay close to your body throughout the exercise.

Move: As you exhale, slowly curl the dumbbell up, bending your elbows and rotating the weight to palms up, bringing it almost to shoulder height. Inhale and slowly lower the weight back down.

Focus: It should take about six seconds to complete one repetition. Do eight to twelve repetitions.

Comments: Watch that your shoulders stay down and back when performing this exercise. It's a common error to see the shoulders roll forward and elevate. Another common mistake is letting momentum take over the exercise—make sure you stay controlled, and don't swing the weight.

Variations: Biceps curls can also be done in a hammer grip (thumbs up), which changes the focus of the exercise in the forearm and the wrist. Another variation that changes the angle of work is having your palms down (reverse grip).

Plank Forearm Hover

Targets: Shoulders, abdominals, hips, and legs.

Setup: Kneel on all fours with your knees under your hips and hands under your shoulders. Drop down to your forearms and walk your feet back until you're on the balls of your feet, pressing your heels back with your knees straight.

Move: Holding this position, focus on pulling your abdominals up and in (think of them as a hammock that's pulling your center up to your spine). Work your posture—widen your collarbones, press your shoulder blades down toward your waist, lengthen your neck. Breathe deeply, holding this position for up to half a minute.

Focus: There should not be any sag in your lower back (as you fatigue and your muscles begin to give up, watch that this doesn't happen—lower yourself down for a recovery rest). Your head should also be in alignment with your spine and not sagging.

Comments: Once you've mastered this exercise, you can try lifting one leg off the floor, and then the other. This is a great exercise to make many muscle groups work harmoniously together. You can modify it to be on your knees rather than your toes. It's more beneficial, however, to hold for a shorter time in the plank from your toes than to do a longer plank from your knees.

Triceps Kickback with Hip Hinge

Targets: The back of your upper arm (triceps).

Setup: Stand tall, with your knees slightly bent and hip distance apart. Hinge at the hips so that your back stays straight. This will engage your back muscles while you perform the exercise. Holding a dumbbell in each hand, lift your arms until your elbows are slightly behind you, palms facing in.

Move: As you exhale, slowly straighten your elbow until your arm is straight (your elbow should not lock straight). Pause at the top of the movement, inhale, and return to the start position.

Focus: Make sure you keep your shoulders away from your ears, with your shoulder blades pressed down toward your waist and pulled in toward your spine. Lengthen your neck. Pull your abdominals up and in. It's very important that you keep your back straight and not allow your spine to flex.

Comments: Since this position incorporates back and core strength, you could modify it to be a one-at-a-time triceps kickback, using a chair to support the forward hip hinge.

One-Arm Double-Bell Row

Targets: Sides of your upper back (latissimus dorsi, trapezius), back of your shoulder (posterior deltoid), front of your upper arm (biceps), postural muscle near your shoulder blades (rhomboids).

Setup: Stand tall with your knees slightly bent and hip distance apart. Take a large step back with your right leg and hinge forward at the hips, keeping your back straight. You can either use your nonworking hand to give you support by placing it on your thigh, or incorporate back strength and stability by holding your form in the hip hinge with no assistance. With both dumbbells (or a heavy bell) in one hand, lower the weights toward the floor, almost straightening your elbow, keeping it tucked in close to your side. Pull your shoulder blades together, press them down toward your waist, and keep them there throughout the exercise.

Move: As you exhale, bend your right arm at the elbow and pull the weight up until your upper arm is parallel to the floor (or a little beyond) and your elbow forms a right angle. Inhale and slowly return to the start position. Do eight to twelve repetitions on each arm.

Focus: Keep the weight close to your side throughout the exercise. Keep your neck lengthened, your collarbones open and wide.

Back Flye

Targets: Upper back (trapezius, rhomboids) and the rear of your shoulders (posterior deltoid).

Setup: Stand tall with your knees slightly bent and hip distance apart. Hinge forward at the hips, keeping your back straight and your neck lengthened. Your elbows will be slightly bent, your arms extended out in front of you.

Move: Exhale, squeeze your shoulder blades together, and slowly lift your arms out to the sides until they are slightly higher than shoulder level, feeling your shoulder blades press toward your spine. Pause, inhale, and lower the weights with control. Do eight to twelve repetitions.

Focus: Your arms should lift directly to your sides, not behind you. Remember to keep your shoulder blades actively pressed toward your spine throughout the exercise. At the completion of the exercise, allow your shoulder blades to widen away from your spine to get a full range of motion.

Comments: Try this exercise without weights at first to feel the movement of the shoulder blades. Use light weights at first so you don't compromise your range of motion.

Military Press (Overhead Press)

Targets: Shoulders (medial deltoids), arms (biceps), and upper back and neck area (upper trapezius).

Setup: Stand tall with your feet hip width apart and your knees slightly bent. Engage your abdominals by pulling them up and in, keeping your spine straight. Widen your collarbones, lengthen your neck, and draw your shoulders down and away from your ears. Hold the dumbbells at shoulder height with your elbows bent and pointing out to the sides, and your palms facing front or inward (modified).

Move: Exhale and straighten your arms (keep your elbows unlocked), pushing the dumbbells over and slightly in front of your head. Pause, inhale, and slowly lower back to the start position. Do eight to twelve repetitions.

Focus: Keep your abdominals pulled in and your torso active to avoid arching or collapsing in the back. Keep your neck muscles lengthened and your shoulders pressed down away from your ears, even as you push the weight overhead.

Comments: If this exercise bothers your shoulders, try modifying the hand position from facing front to facing inward (which externally rotates the shoulder joint)—or avoid the exercise.

Push-Ups (Three Levels)

Targets: Chest (pectoralis major), front of the shoulders (anterior deltoid), back of the upper arms (triceps); when performed on your toes, your abdominals (especially transverse) and buttocks will stabilize.

Setup: Level 1: Kneel on the ground with your arms lined up so that your wrists are directly beneath your shoulders and your fingertips are straight ahead of you, turned in slightly. Walk your hands forward until your body forms as straight a line as possible from your knees up to your shoulders. Keep your neck in line with your spine. Levels 2 and 3: Do the setup above, except that you'll walk out to a straight body balancing on your toes.

Move: Level 1: Inhale, bending your elbows, and lower your body down until your chest nears the floor. Pause, exhale, and press back up to the start position. Level 2: Inhale, bending your elbows, and lower your body down until your chest nears the floor. Now drop your knees to the level 1 position, and push up to the start position. Level 3: Inhale, bending your elbows, and lower your body down until your chest nears the floor. Pause, exhale, and push back to the start position.

Focus: Hold your abdominal muscles in tight so that your body is in a straight line as you lower it. Don't let your body sag as you fatigue. If you can't lower your body down in the push-up in level 1, start with a quarter push-up, and gradually progress to going lower. The push-up should be completed slowly, controlled, with no momentum.

Comments: Once you can easily perform eight to twelve push-ups in level 1, try a couple in level 2, then complete the set in level 1. Once you can perform eight to twelve push-ups in level 2, try the first couple in a set at level 3, then completing the set in level 2 or 1.

House for a Mouse

Targets: Transverse abdominis.

Setup: Lie prone on the floor.

Move: Draw your navel toward your spine. You should feel your stomach area drawing off the floor.

Focus: Your pubic bone and ribs should not move. The buttocks should not contract.

Comments: This is an exercise to learn to use this muscle. The spine doesn't flex, as it does in a crunch when you use the rectus abdominis. This muscle, the transverse abdominis, is an important postural muscle. You should be using this muscle in every exercise you perform. As your body awareness increases, this will become second nature to you, and it'll get easier as you get stronger.

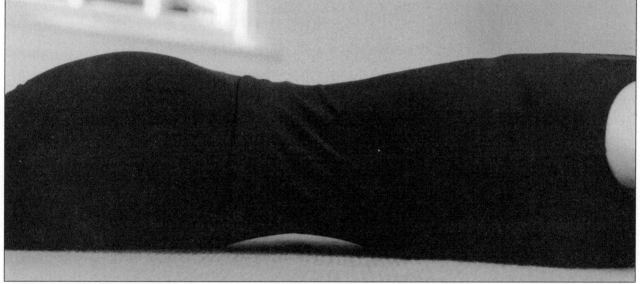

Tabletop Alternating Legs*

Targets: All abdominal muscles (rectus abdominis, obliques, transverse abdominis).

Setup: Lie on your back with your knees over your hips and your feet at hip height. Funnel your ribs down toward the pelvis, and pull your navel toward your spine. Widen your collarbones, relaxing your throat.

Move: Alternate lowering your legs toward the floor. The nonmoving knee stays over your hip (it should not creep in toward your chest). Work up to about eight to twelve reps on each leg.

Focus: Your pelvis should not move at all—no rotation or tipping. You should not feel your tailbone move toward the floor or your back arch. Your ribs should not flare open; they must stay funneled shut. If any of these things happen (you lose form), the intensity is too hard, and you should keep your legs tighter toward the torso.

Comments: The positioning of your knees dictates the intensity. The farther your knees are from your center (away from your chest), the harder the intensity. If your back arches, the abdominals have ceased to be the working muscle, and the exercise then becomes risky. Because there's no spinal flexion involved in this exercise, it's a good option for women who know they have osteoporosis in their spine and have been told by their doctor that they should not do abdominal curls (you should still check with your doctor).

Variation: Once you have mastered alternating legs, you can increase the intensity by lowering both legs to the floor at the same time. Make sure your back doesn't arch, your ribs stay funneled down, and your navel stays pressed toward your spine.

*No spinal flexion—a good option for those who know they have osteoporosis in their spine.

Leg Slides*

Targets: All abdominal muscles (rectus abdominis, obliques, transverse abdominis).

Setup: Lie on your back with your knees bent, your feet on the floor, and your hips slightly externally rotated.

Move: Slide your feet in toward yourself, and back out to almost straight.

Focus: Your ribs are funneled down toward your pelvis, your navel pressed toward your spine. Your hips stay stationary (no rotation or tipping of the pelvis), and your back doesn't arch—it stays quiet and in neutral.

Comments: Once you master this exercise, there are two more intensity levels. The next level of intensity is to lighten the touch of your feet on the floor. Your feet will barely touch the floor, just skimming it as they move in and out. The hardest intensity level is with your feet entirely off the floor, moving in and out. On all intensity levels, it's imperative that your back doesn't arch, that your ribs stay closed and down, and that your hips don't rotate.

*No spinal flexion—a good option for those who know they have osteoporosis in their spine.

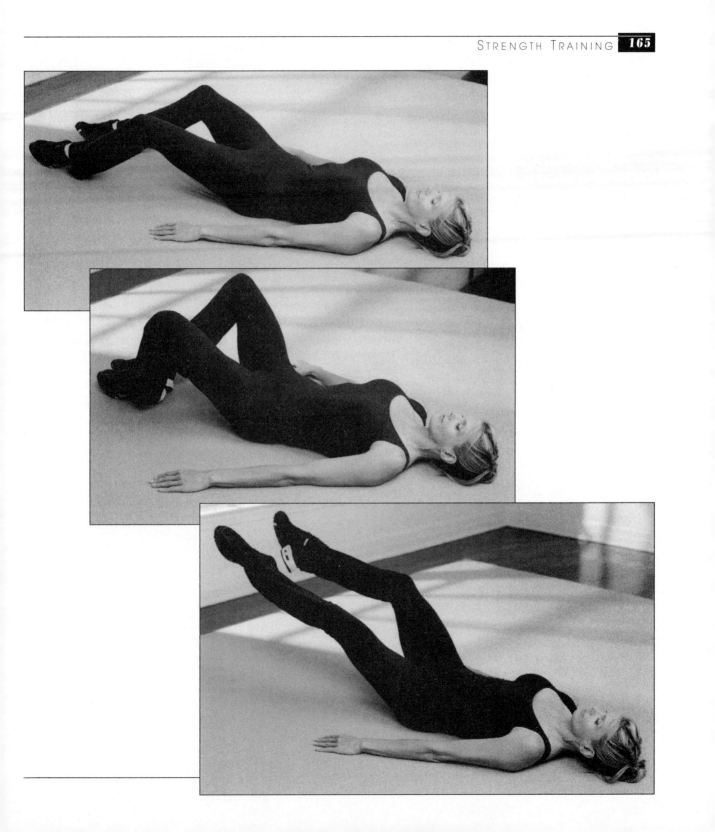

Alternating Leg Lifts*

Targets: All abdominal muscles (rectus abdominis, obliques, transverse abdominis).

Setup: Lie on your back with your knees slightly bent, and your hips slightly externally rotated.

Move: Keeping your hips and back from arching and moving, alternate lifting your legs off the floor. Keep your ribs down tight, and your navel pressed toward your spine.

Focus: It's very important that you don't arch your back.

Comments: When you get strong enough, try lifting your foot off the floor before the other foot touches down. If your back arches when you try this, either bend your knees a little more, or stick to the first level a while longer.

*No spinal flexion—a good option for those who know they have osteoporosis in their spine.

One Hundred

Targets: All abdominal muscles (rectus abdominis, obliques, transverse abdominis).

Setup: Lie on your back and draw your rib cage down toward your pelvis, lifting your shoulders and head. Widen your shoulder blades, and keep your shoulders pressed down away from your ears. Pull your navel down toward your spine. Lift your legs either to a tabletop position (knees over hips, feet as high as knees), or to straight knees directly over your hips. Inhale. As you exhale, lower your legs as far as you can without having any arching of the back, movement of the pelvis, or release of the rib cage.

Move: Hover your arms right over the floor and pump them palms down, as if you were lightly splashing water. Inhale for five seconds, then exhale for five seconds as you hold the leg positioning and pump your arms. Do ten sets of five seconds inhaling, five seconds exhaling.

Focus: Inhale through your nose, exhale through your lips. Keep your ribs knit close to the top of your pelvis, and keep your low back from arching. Elongate through your arms and shoulders. Lengthen your neck and relax your throat.

Comments: If your neck gets tired, try placing one hand behind your head to support it, taking turns with your arms as you complete the exercise, or take a full recovery break, then try some more sets after a rest. As you get stronger, you'll be able to take your legs farther away from your center, and go with straight knees.

Obliques Using Lateral Flexion

Targets: All abdominal muscles (rectus abdominis, obliques, transverse abdominis).

Setup: Lie on your back, with your knees slightly bent and in slight external rotation.

Move: Do one abdominal curl, bringing your rib cage to your pelvis, and stay up. Stay high as you reach your right arm toward the inside of your right knee—bringing your right ribs toward the top of the right side of your pelvis. Hike your right hip toward your right ribs. Stay high as you laterally flex back to the center position. Repeat eight to twelve times on the right, then on the left.

Focus: Once you do the initial curl, stay up throughout the lateral flexion moves.

Comments: When you reach to the right, you should feel the obliques on your right, and vice versa.

Boat (with Assisted Lift into Intensity with Arms)

Targets: Rectus abdominis, transverse abdominis.

Setup: Lie on your back, and lift your feet up to a tabletop position.

Move: Curl up as high as you can go. Using your hands, grab your thighs and boost yourself a little higher—lift up one or two vertebrae. Slowly let go of your thighs, staying as high as you were. Keep your rib cage pulled down toward your navel as you move your arms back over your head. Your low back should stay down toward the floor and not arch. Hold that position for a count of five. Repeat six to twelve times.

Focus: When your arms move back over your head, fight to keep your ribs down and your low back in the same position it was in when you were in the curl.

Comments: This exercise gets more difficult as the tabletop position of your legs moves away from your center, or you perform the exercise with straight legs.

Chapter 9

Cardiovascular Exercise

*Careful grooming may take twenty years off a woman's age,
but you can't fool a long flight of stairs.*
—*Marlene Dietrich*

Is there ever a day so hectic, or a mood so dark, that it can't be improved by a brisk walk in the fresh air? Whatever may have gotten you moving in years past, perimenopause offers a whole new inducement: psychological rejuvenation. Studies show that women who exercise regularly improve their sense of well-being and report feeling less bothered by perimenopausal symptoms. It just makes sense that being more fit makes you feel more in charge of your body again.

Benefits of Cardiovascular Exercise

Cardiovascular (aerobic) exercise, in particular, conveys a number of benefits that are especially welcome at this time of life:

- Improves your blood cholesterol levels, by reducing LDLs and raising HDLs
- Stimulates your bones to remain strong
- Helps you manage weight by burning calories and raising your metabolism

- Provides a surge of mood-elevating endorphins
- Improves your sleep
- Sparks up your sex life by improving your energy and mood
- Improves balance
- Boosts self-esteem and increases your feeling of being in control

There are lots of fun ways to develop cardiovascular fitness—everything from running or jogging to tennis, aerobic dance, stair climbing, kickboxing, and more. In this chapter, I'm going to focus on the simplest and most accessible—walking. I'll show you how to get a powerful cardio workout with my *Moving Through Menopause* Walking Program, using the special intensity-boosting techniques of *periodization* and *interval training*.

Solving the Energy Shortage

Women often say to me: "Kathy, I know I need to exercise, but when you're having hot flashes and not sleeping, you just don't have the energy." As someone who's having sleep problems herself, I can relate. So where *do* you find the energy to exercise when your body is under so much stress? Here are some suggestions:

- **Start slowly.** The first secret is to do it gradually. Your top priority should be to get *some* kind of routine going, no matter how small. A daily ten-minute walk around the neighborhood is far better than a full-bore gym workout you never do. Start with a small, easy routine you can be *consistent* with.
- **Conserve energy.** Match your intensity level to your energy level. Scale back your workout on the days you're low on energy and seize the days you feel strong. Remember, even a stroll will get your circulation going; you don't have to break records every day.
- **Accept whatever level you can achieve.** Don't give up. If you slack off, start again. For many people, fitness is a lifetime of starting again.

That's fine. Over time, you'll still spend a higher percentage of your life being active.

- **Schedule your workouts for the times you most need them.** Almost everyone feels more relaxed, alert, and alive after exercise. If you can figure out at what point in your day you most need to recharge your batteries, and make it a habit to work out then, you'll find yourself looking forward to it.
- **Harness your emotional voltage.** Use your workout as a release from feelings of stress, frustration, or anger. Channeling these emotions into strenuous exercise is like connecting to a power source. Not only will you find yourself pushing harder than you ever imagined, but you'll feel your negative emotions transformed into feelings of power, excitement, and passion.

Kathy's *Moving Through Menopause* Walking Program

A walking program can be as simple as just going out for a brisk stroll a few times a week. As long as you're consistent about doing it, that's fine. Eventually, though, your body adapts to the demands of a steady pace, and it's hard to progress any farther. That's why my walking program is based on periodization—a valuable tool to help you get more out of your exercise program. Consult a doctor before beginning this or any cardio program.

Periodization

Periodization is a proven, scientific method of training that elite athletes use to "peak" just before a big event. It's especially useful if you've hit a plateau—the place where, though you continue to work out, you stop seeing progress. It works by varying one or more of the three key aspects of your workout—length, intensity, and activity. By changing what you ask your body to do, periodization challenges you so you keep making fitness progress.

We'll be using walking as our aerobic activity, and each week we'll adjust either the duration or intensity of our workouts. Later, if you want, you can adapt the program to any other activity.

Intensity Ranges

Since part of the periodization concept involves varying our intensity, we need a way to quantify how much effort we're expending at a given moment. I use a one-through-ten scale of perceived exertion (see box).

At the low end is the "comfort zone" most people gravitate to—a level well below their potential maximum. At the high end of the scale is your anaerobic threshold, the point beyond which your heart and lungs are unable to keep sufficient oxygen moving to the muscles, and you're forced to stop. Naturally, you can't work continuously at an eight or nine. But you'll get more results—and have more fun—by working up and down through the *full* range, rather than just plodding along in that comfort zone. That's what our walking program will do.

My *Moving Through Menopause* Walking Program consists of three walks, each with its own distinct intensity profile. We'll start with the basic level.

Walk I: The Flat Line—Just Get in Gear and Go!

This walk is designed to get you off the couch and onto your feet. It will build stamina and endurance, as well as provide a good base from which you can progress to the next two walking levels.

Depending on your level of fitness, you'll be walking anywhere from ten to sixty minutes at a comfortable, steady pace at which you can carry on a conversation. Before you start the program, determine the time it takes you to walk 1 mile, so that you have a baseline against which to measure your progress. To do this, simply find a comfortable route, mark off a mile, and record the time it takes to walk it at an easy pace.

Begin Walk I with an easy five-minute warm-up, comparable to a strolling pace. Then increase your pace by a notch. This is your "steady-state" pace, and should correspond to an intensity level of a four to five (see box). If you feel you want to do more—or as your endurance improves—increase your walk by five to ten minutes, keeping the intensity moderate.

Continue doing Walk I until you can complete a mile in twenty minutes or less.

5 minutes warm-up pace

| 10–50 minutes steady-state pace | ◄—— (increase your time as your stamina improves)

5 minutes cool-down pace

Walk II: The Wave—Cycle Up and Down Through Varying Intensities

This walk uses aerobic intervals (bursts of higher-intensity work) to get you to work a little harder for short amounts of time within your twenty- to thirty-minute workout. Doing so will increase your endurance and fitness, and burn a greater number of calories than Walk I.

5–10 minutes warm-up pace

| 3 minutes at 5–6 |
| 3 minutes at 7–8 | ◄—— (work up to doing 3 cycles)
| 2 minutes at 8–9 |

5–10 minutes of cool-down

Walk III: The Peak—Take the Challenge

Walk III is a real challenge; I recommend you not attempt it until you've developed a basic level of fitness with Walks I and II. In Walk III, the pace steadily accelerates in two-minute increments until you reach your maximum. Then you drop back to level 5 and begin the climb again.

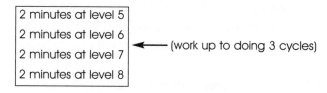

5 minutes warm-up pace

| 2 minutes at level 5 |
| 2 minutes at level 6 |
| 2 minutes at level 7 |
| 2 minutes at level 8 |

← (work up to doing 3 cycles)

5–10 minutes of cool-down

HOW HARD AM I WORKING?

Instead of having to continually stop to take my pulse, I like to gauge my intensity using a ten-point scale. The numbers are associated with specific physical sensations. Here's how it feels to work your way up the scale:

Levels 1–4: Very Easy

A strolling pace, suitable for warm-up or cool-down.

Levels 4–5: Cruising

This is your "steady-state" pace. You can easily carry on a conversation.

Levels 5–6: Moderate

You're pushing slightly, and feeling invigorated. You're breathing harder, but can still carry on a conversation.

Levels 7–8: Hard

You're starting to perspire, getting a little winded. You're feeling some fatigue in your legs, and it's difficult to speak.

Levels 9–10: Killer

This feels like the homestretch of a race. You're breathing hard, and there's a burning sensation in your muscles.

How Much, How Often?

The three walks in this program each place different demands on your body. By cycling among them and adjusting the duration to match your fitness level, you can continue challenging yourself and keep the gains coming. Follow the guidelines below and increase your time as you develop stamina.

First, determine your fitness level to decide where you're going to start:

	JUST STARTING OUT	MODERATELY ACTIVE	VERY ACTIVE
HOW OFTEN	2–3 times/week	3–4 times/week	4–6 times/week
HOW LONG	10–20 minutes	20–30 minutes	30–60 minutes

Then begin the walks, progressing over the course of six weeks as shown:

Week 1	Walk I
Week 2	Walk I
Week 3	Walk II
Week 4	Walk II
Week 5	Walk III
Week 6	Walk III

After week six, repeat the cycle starting with Walk I, this time doing longer-duration walks. For additional variety, you can adapt this plan to other activities like running, or to aerobic equipment such as a treadmill, stairs, or stationary bicycle. Experiment with different activities to find your favorites.

Set Yourself Up for Success

In many ways, both physical and spiritual, walking outdoors comes pretty close to being the perfect exercise. Still, there are times when it's pouring or snowing, or times you just need a change. So to make sure nothing derails your program, it's a good idea to have some alternative activities in mind.

ESSENTIAL TECHNIQUE POINTS FOR WALKING

- **Posture**

Stand tall; imagine a string coming from the top of your head pulling you up. Then tilt your body forward slightly from the ankles, not the hips or waist. Don't arch your lower back or stick your butt out. Keep your spine in a neutral position by contracting your abdominals.

- **Head Position**

Don't tilt your head from side to side, and don't drop your chin forward. Your eyes should focus straight ahead and not on your feet, so you don't strain your neck.

- **Shoulders**

Your shoulders should be down and back; open your chest for easier, deeper breathing. As you walk, check your shoulders regularly. Are you slouching? Are your shoulders creeping up toward your ears?

- **Arms**

Let your arms swing freely, but with purpose. This improves balance, increases circulation, and burns more calories. Swing your arms forward, not across your body. Imagine your body on a clock face, viewed from the side, with your head at twelve o'clock. Your arms should swing from seven o'clock (just behind your hips) to four o'clock (about belly button height).

- **Feet**

Strike the ground with your heel and let your foot roll forward naturally. At the end of your stride, really push off with your toes, to propel your body forward. Use a stride length that's comfortable for you. Don't overstride.

To modify your technique when walking at greater speeds:

- **Arms**

Since your arms and legs work in unison, your legs can't speed up until your arms do. To get your arms pumping more quickly, start by putting a 90-degree bend in your elbows, holding your hands in a loose fist. Swing forward, not side to side, keeping your elbows close to your sides.

- **Feet**

Use the same rolling heel–toe motion as at lower speeds, but concentrate on actively pulling up your toes as your legs swing forward. At faster paces, if you don't pull up your toes, you'll start catching them on the ground.

In choosing alternative exercises, remember that one of the key benefits of exercise at midlife is bone health. Bones respond most readily to load-bearing exercises, which increase the amount of weight the skeleton supports, either through impact or by using actual weights. The best cardio exercises for your bones are the higher-impact choices, such as running, jogging, and racquet sports, or medium-impact choices such as walking or stair climbing. Nonimpact activities like swimming and cycling are fine if you can't do higher-impact activities because of joint pain, but they're not the best ways to target your bones. In general, choose the highest-impact exercises you're comfortable with, but be sensitive to your joints and stop if you feel any pain.

I suggest you begin by completing the six-week walking program I've described. Then, if you like, branch out into other activities from there.

Take Your Soul for a Walk

Finally, remember that walking offers more than fitness, and don't overlook the power it has to lift your spirit. Whether it's an after-dinner stroll with the family or a weekend hike with friends, simply taking frequent, short walks for pleasure and relaxation is a wonderful habit to adopt into your life. One of my favorite times is early morning. I may have had the world's worst night, but rolling out of bed at sunrise—straight out of my dreams and into the fresh air for a half-hour walk—always brings me back to life.

So when the blues come after you, just make yourself a moving target. Get out there and walk!

Chapter 10

Rejuvenation

Adopt the pace of nature, her secret is patience.
—Ralph Waldo Emerson

Stress can be a killer, especially for the perimenopausal woman. When the body senses stress, our adrenal glands react by pumping out the hormones adrenaline and cortisol. Too much of these chemicals can wreak havoc on the body, triggering hot flashes and menstrual irregularities, and worsening hypertension. Mood swings, fatigue, fuzzy thinking, and sleep problems can all be exacerbated. Excess weight begins to accumulate in the abdominal region. Years of this can deplete your adrenal glands—your major source of postmenopausal estrogen.

Yet strange as it sounds, stress is a necessary part of life. A certain amount of stress motivates us; it helps focus our minds and keeps us productive. Finding the perfect balance isn't easy; in fact, judging by how we manage our lives, most of us seem to have a "stress wish"—we overcommit ourselves, we worry, we're self-critical. And then when stress strikes, we often resort to things that make it worse.

Escape Versus Rejuvenation

When was the last time you heard yourself say: "I am so tense and worn out—what I need is a brisk walk, a healthy dinner, a warm bath, and a good night's sleep"? Be honest. Although I can guarantee this prescription would be wonderfully restorative, I'll bet most of us would rank it well below a slice of chocolate cheesecake and a few hours of shopping.

Amazingly, most people don't have a clue what will actually make them feel better. Instead, they run to short-term fixes—excessive alcohol and drugs, fattening "comfort food," hours of TV, spending sprees, destructive sexual affairs. They reach for an anesthetic rather than a rejuvenator.

I certainly understand the urge to escape now and then. Some forms of escape can be very nourishing—a great book, or a delicious bottle of wine shared with friends.

But there are constructive, positive ways to unwind that do more than just mask your stress: They *rejuvenate* you—fill you up spiritually and return you to the world feeling stronger, calmer, and more in control.

In this chapter, I'll share some of the strategies I use to relax and recharge.

Managing Your Spiritual Bank Account

Every day, our sense of inner peace vies with the stresses outside. I think of this as a spiritual bank account: Our healthy, self-nurturing habits build it up, and stress siphons it down.

At times when we're feeling especially good, it's human nature to take on too much, stay up too late, and drive ourselves too hard. This is like overspending when there's money burning a hole in your pocket. Before you know it, you've splurged the energy you had and are left without reserves.

The trick is not to wait until you're overdrawn. Successful stress management means constantly monitoring your stress level and making daily deposits to your spiritual bank account, by doing nurturing, rejuvenating things.

When you know you're going to be under pressure, look ahead and see what you can do to make it more manageable. For example, when I have a particularly stress-filled couple of weeks, I plot out breathing spaces: the good meals I plan to eat, the yoga classes I'll attend—even the nap I'll take on the weekend.

In addition, I have a short list of "emergency" remedies—guaranteed rejuvenators that I can count on anytime I'm starting to feel just the tiniest bit frayed or vulnerable. They're not designed to solve all my problems in a split second; their purpose is to reinforce the habit of making self-nurturing choices. Each one is a little spiritual oasis. After reading mine, try to come up with some of your own. They don't have to be complicated; a few deep breaths at a key moment can change your whole state of mind.

Kathy's Favorite Emergency Remedies

• Switching the car radio to a classical station—rock music and talk radio are designed to stir you up; sometimes that's one stimulant too many.

• A cup of herbal chai tea at my favorite teahouse—this gives me fifteen or twenty minutes of restful quiet time while I sit and drink it.

• A hot bath (just be aware that hot baths can be a hot-flash trigger).

• A yoga class.

• Deep, rhythmic breathing.

• Cooking.

• Juggling—I love it; it forces me to clear my thoughts and be in the present!

• _____

• _____

• _____

Stress is normal, but if you let it escalate and peak, it can start costing you sleep, or worse. That's why it's your responsibility to find ways to take the edge off.

Creating Sanctuary

Your home should be a refuge from tension and care. How many of us can say that's the case? Often, we endure the stress of a chaotic home environment just because we've grown used to it. We forget that we're free to create any kind of surroundings we can imagine. I'm not talking about an expensive kitchen remodel or add-on. I'm talking about the little things you can do to make your environment more soothing and harmonious.

For me, the quest for serenity has meant moving my business out of the house, and not answering phones during dinner. It's meant more family time. More music and less TV. Reading books with my kids instead of always watching videos. Once you start brainstorming, there are literally hundreds of possibilities. Some of them might involve changes in the physical environment, while others might address lifestyle habits or family interactions. All of this adds up to less stress.

How many things can you think of? Make a list of ways to make your home a more comfortable, peaceful, and nurturing place. Here are a few ideas to get you going, with space to start adding your own:

- Plant a small area in your yard with flowers and fragrant herbs, with a chair where you can sit and unwind.
- Install double-glazed windows in your bedroom for a more restful sleep.
- Have your house professionally cleaned every now and then to restore a sense of order.
- Use more terms of endearment with your family.

- _____

- _____

- _____

Quiet Time

One of the basic antidotes to stress is to schedule a little personal quiet time every day—time to breathe, to daydream, to listen to nature, and feel your batteries recharging. I like to take a few moments first thing in the morning to meditate or write in my journal. I also try to schedule a buffer at the end of the day, to help the transition toward sleep.

You can do various things with your quiet time. Here are some ideas.

Meditation

Meditation need not be part of a religious or philosophical practice. It can simply be a discipline of refocusing the mind. Actually, we do a lot of meditation in our daily life without realizing it. Trouble is, we tend to meditate on the negative—another word for that might be *worry.* Our tape recorder gets stuck on one track, like a bad DJ, and negative ideas circulate in our heads, thoughts like *I'm not a good person* or *I'm not doing anything with my life.*

In the simplest sense, meditation can help banish negative thoughts by clearing your mind entirely. Another way is to focus on a positive idea. It's not always easy to erase negative thought patterns, but meditation can at least help you become more conscious of them, and that's the first step. As you work to clear your mind (or to hold positive images in your mind), you may still hear negative messages surfacing. When that happens, simply notice them and refocus. Some people find it useful to say or think the word *stop* when negative thoughts start to play.

Nature Meditation

One of my favorite ways to change my mental state is to meditate deeply on a part of nature. Take five minutes to look closely at a flower. Study the details of its texture and the structure. When you do this, you develop a sense of reverence. The flower becomes a little miracle. You begin to see how complete and fully alive the natural world is at all levels. Meditating on nature can be calming, fascinating, and inspiring all at once.

Gratitude Meditation

I like to do this first thing in the morning, to get my day moving on a positive track. Simply spend a few minutes meditating on all the things in your life that you're thankful for.

Breathing Meditation

Slow, deep breathing is one of the best stress busters there is. Focus your attention on the breath entering your body, your breath flowing out, and the spaces in between. Several minutes of this can lower your pulse, reduce your blood pressure, and relax much of the muscular tension in your body.

Journaling

Occasionally throughout this book, I've suggested journal exercises to focus your attention on various issues and questions. Journaling can serve as a powerful stress reducer by providing a safe place to express feelings and organize your thoughts.

A second type of journaling is *automatic writing,* in which you set a timer for five minutes and write whatever comes to mind. Don't worry about clarity or continuity—just write your thoughts down as they come. This technique is very useful for breaking through emotional blocks and getting in touch with your feelings. It can also be a wonderful stimulus to creativity. This form of journal writing is a great way to complete the dream process in the morning, or clear your mind at night.

Let It Out

Most of us shy away from feelings of loneliness, sadness, or anger. We spend a lot of time and energy trying to "hold it together," while the feelings are percolating just under the surface. As a result, you may find yourself breaking down or snapping at people at inappropriate times.

Crying is my salvation. I love to close the door to my bathroom and just let it all out—I sob and moan and pound my fists like a baby. And almost magically, the cloud of despair lifts. Within about five or ten minutes I've gotten it out, and the situation that seemed so devastating now feels under control. I know crying seems like a basic response that needs no discussion. But here's a technique from my friend and psychologist Ann Christie, designed to help you really open up to the feelings that are trying to surface.

Controlled Crying

When you feel that tension rising in the pit of your stomach, create a safe place and time to release it. Go someplace where you feel comfortable and secure and won't be disturbed. Then let it go: Cry with your whole body.

Experiment with bringing more focus and power to the experience by speaking your feelings out loud, in simple, direct terms: *I'm lonely, I hate my life,* and so on. Keep going until you can't cry another tear. I guarantee this will change your state. If you wish, discuss any insights you gained this way in your journal.

It takes courage to open up to the full force of your feelings, but it's the only way to move through them.

Progressive Relaxation

Progressive relaxation is a powerful way to lead your mind out of negative thought patterns. It's usually done by listening to a recorded message that guides you through the process. Progressive relaxation tapes are one of my favorite techniques when I can't sleep at night: I keep my headphones right by the bed so I don't even have to turn on the light.

There are many good progressive relaxation tapes available. If you want, you can make your own using the script I've provided in the Appendix.

Yoga

Cutting stress is one of the best weapons against midlife problems, and yoga provides the perfect combination of techniques to accomplish the job. By toning the nervous system and improving circulation, yoga exercise can pull you back from emotional plunges and rejuvenate your energy supply. It clears your mind and puts your body at ease so that you can concentrate during the day and sleep at night. Certain postures affect the endocrine and reproductive systems, which can help balance erratic hormonal shifts and awaken the sex center.

In addition, yoga lifts your spine and lubricates your joints and muscles, helping eliminate low back pain and body aches. Most of all, it gives you the flexibility and strength that keep you young and vital, so you can really enjoy the new freedoms that come after menopause.

Wisdom Pose (Child's Pose)

1. Standing on your knees and shins, bring your knees hip distance apart and your toes together. Relax your hips back onto your heels and lay your chest out over your thighs. Extend your arms onto the floor at your sides.

2. Completely relax everywhere and allow your forehead, shoulders, belly, and hips to release down toward the floor. Bring your awareness to your breath, feeling the simple and complete flow of each inhale and exhale. Let your breath gradually deepen, paying more attention to the beginning of each inhale, the ending of each exhale, and the quiet spaces in between. With each inhale, feel more space across your back and shoulders and in your belly; with each exhale, let your body drop down more toward the floor, feeling more and more calm.

3. Hold for two to five minutes or longer.

Benefits: Relaxes and releases pressure in the entire body; massages and stimulates the abdominal organs; soothing, calming, and rejuvenating; promotes a sense of ease and tranquillity.

Dog and Cat Tilts

1. Place yourself on all fours, with your knees directly below your hips and your wrists directly below your shoulders. Spread your fingers apart, opening your palms and pressing the entire span of your palms, knuckles, and fingers firmly against the floor.

2. As you inhale, tilt your pelvis forward, causing your sitting bones to lift as you draw your shoulders back, extend your chest, and gaze forward and up (Dog Tilt).

3. As you exhale, reverse this movement, drawing your tailbone down and under you while pressing more firmly through your hands and rounding your spine up toward the ceiling (Cat Tilt).

4. Continue for five more cycles, feeling your breath initiate each movement, gradually deepening the two stretches.

5. After five cycles, relax back into the Wisdom Pose for three slow breaths. Relax completely, feeling your breath and cultivating a feeling of deep relaxation.

Benefits: Awakens breath and spine; stimulates spinal fluid; stimulates the digestive tract; loosens the neck and shoulders; gently stimulates back and abdominal muscles; awakens the spirit and creates a feeling of inner connection with your body and breath.

Bridge Pose

1. Lie on your back, bend your knees, and draw your heels in. Lay your arms at your sides.

2. Take a deep breath, feeling your side ribs and rib cage expand.

3. Slowly exhale, feeling your ribs release. As your breath flows out, allow your belly to sink, gently pressing your spine to the floor and causing your tailbone to tilt up slightly. This tilting action initiates your movement into the Bridge Pose.

4. Once you've exhaled completely, press into your heels and lift your hips as high as you comfortably can. Bring your arms together under you, extended straight with fingers interlaced. Rock from side to side, drawing your shoulders together to relieve pressure on your neck. Hold for five breaths.

5. Keep pressing your heels firmly down into the floor; this will keep your hips extended toward the ceiling. Press your buttocks toward your knees, thereby lengthening and protecting your lower back. Focus the pressure on the inner edges of your feet to keep your knees aligned directly over your ankles, and to keep your inner thighs relaxing toward the floor and prevent tension in the sacrum. Keep pressing down through your shoulders, elbows, and wrists, lifting your chest toward your chin.

6. Hold for five breaths. Then unclasp your hands and slowly roll down, one vertebra at a time, with your sacrum the last to touch the floor. Keep your feet in place, let your knees come together, and completely relax for a few breaths. Repeat two more times.

Benefits: Promotes a healthy nervous system, thereby easing tension and generating more energy; stimulates the kidneys and adrenals; stretches the chest, shoulders, abdominals, and thighs. Promotes stronger libido.

Simple Twist

1. Lie on your back with your legs extended. Slowly draw your right knee up toward your right shoulder until you feel resistance. Stay here for a few breaths, using your hands to gradually pull your knee closer to your right shoulder.

2. Extend your right arm onto the floor to your right. Keeping your shoulders flat, use your left hand to gently pull your right knee across your body until you feel resistance to the twist. With each inhale, slightly relax away from the point of resistance; with each exhale, pull toward the resistance. Continue for five complete cycles of breath.

3. Draw your knee back up and slowly extend your right leg to the floor. Lie still for a few breaths, feeling the effect of the pose. Repeat on your left side.

Benefits: Relieves pressure on the spine; releases tension in the back and chest; calms and tones internal abdominal organs; stimulates blood circulation; aids digestion.

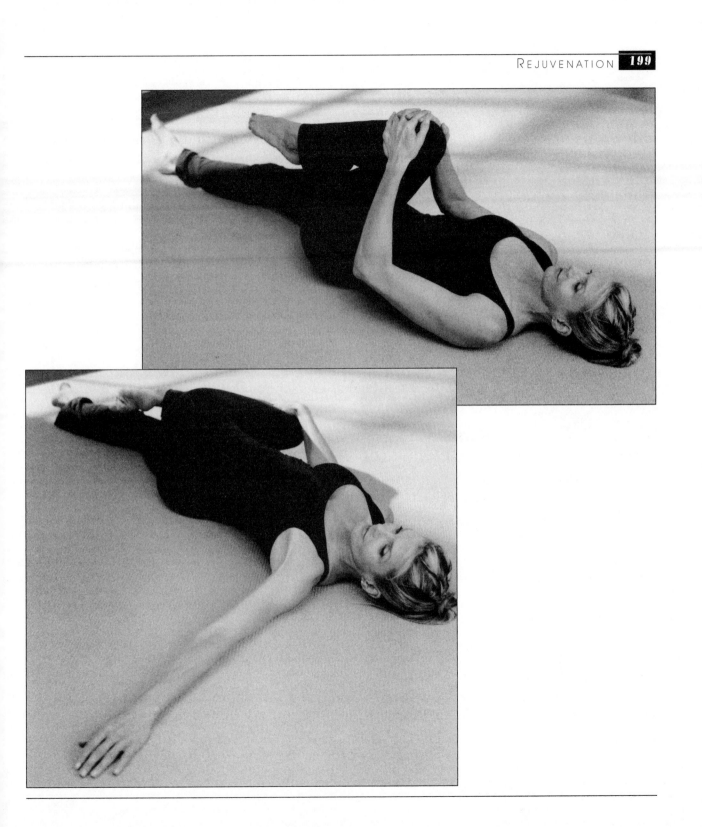

Seated Forward Bend

1. Sit on the floor and extend your legs in front of you, ankles together. If this position is difficult, sit on a firm pillow or bolster until you can maintain straight legs and spine.

2. Firmly press your sitting bones down into the floor, pulling your toes back and pressing the backs of your legs firmly into the floor. Sit as tall as you can. As you inhale, feel your chest lifting and spreading. Maintaining as much length in your spine as you can, slowly lean your torso forward, placing your hands on the floor outside your legs. Keep your sitting bones rooted into the floor.

3. With each inhale, extend farther, lengthening from your belly through your chest while gazing down and keeping the back of your neck long. As you feel more open and flexible, eventually clasp your shins, ankles, feet, or toes. Be sensitive to pressure in your lower back and release if you feel any discomfort. Hold for one to three minutes.

Benefits: Lengthens and strengthens the spine; improves vital energy flow; stimulates abdominal organs, especially the kidneys; refreshes the mind and emotions. The intense stretch of the pelvic region brings more oxygenated blood there, nourishing the reproductive organs and promoting stronger libido. Deeply relaxing and excellent for calming anxiety.

Seated Wide-Angle Forward Bend

1. Sit on the floor and extend your legs in a V shape. If this pose is difficult, sit on a firm pillow or bolster until you can maintain straight legs and spine.

2. Firmly press your sitting bones down into the floor, pulling your toes up and pressing the backs of your legs firmly into the floor. Sit as tall as you can. As you inhale, feel your chest lifting and spreading. Keeping your spine tall, slowly lean forward, bringing your hands, forearms, or chest to the floor in front of you. Keep your sitting bones rooted to the floor.

3. With each inhale, extend farther, lengthening from your belly through your chest while gazing down and keeping the back of your neck long. Be sensitive to pressure in your lower back and release if you feel any sharp sensations in your spine. Hold for one to three minutes.

Benefits: Helps circulate blood properly in the pelvic region; stimulates the ovaries and adrenals; opens the groin; stretches the hamstrings. Deeply calming; good for libido.

Head-to-Knee Pose

1. This pose begins the same as the Seated Forward Bend. Sit on the floor with your legs extended, ankles together. Firmly press your sitting bones into the floor, pulling your toes up and pressing the backs of your legs firmly into the floor. Sit as tall as you can.

2. With as little change in your posture as possible, slide your right heel up to press into your left inner thigh. As you do so, draw your right knee toward the floor. Be sensitive to any pressure in your right knee. Place your hands on the floor just behind your hips to encourage more extension through your spine while keeping your sitting bones pressed firmly into the floor. Slightly turn your torso and chest toward your extended leg.

3. As you inhale, grow taller through your spine and more expansive across your chest. Then exhale and fold forward over your left leg, placing your hands to the sides of your left leg or grasping your left foot. Hold and continue to breathe.

4. With each inhale, lean farther forward, lengthening from your belly through your chest while gazing down and keeping the back of your neck long. As you feel more open and flexible, clasp your shins, ankles, feet, or toes. Be sensitive to pressure in your lower back and release if you feel discomfort in your spine. Hold for one minute. Repeat on the other side.

Benefits: Stretches the legs, relieves tension in the lower back, elongates the spine, opens the hips, stimulates circulation through the spine, torso, and abdominal organs, quiets the mind.

Cobbler Pose

1. Sitting on the floor, draw your heels together, and let your knees drop to the sides. If you find it difficult to maintain a straight spine while positioning yourself on the front edge of your sitting bones, sit on a firm pillow or bolster until you can.

2. Place your hands on the floor behind you and press into the floor. Rise up taller through the core of your body and roll your pelvis more forward, shifting your weight onto the front edge of your sitting bones. Once you can maintain this position without your hands behind you, place your hands on your feet with thumbs on the insides of your feet. Open up the soles of your feet like a book, and continue to hold them.

3. Inhale, extending taller through your spine; then exhale and slowly fold forward. Keep your sitting bones firmly rooted into the floor, drawing your belly toward your toes as you stretch your sternum forward. Focus your attention on your breath, cultivating greater extension through your spine with each inhale, and releasing more deeply into the pose with each exhale. Hold for one to three minutes.

Benefits: Opens the hips, stretches the inner thighs, improves circulation through the hips, legs, and pelvic region, releasing tension deep inside the hips and pelvis while promoting stronger libido.

Shoulderstand (or Half Shoulderstand)

1. Lie on your back. Draw your feet overhead and roll your hips up until your toes reach a chair behind your head. Straighten your legs, press down through the pads of your toes into the floor, and press back through the heels of your feet, stretching your calf muscles.

2. Interlace your fingers behind your back and press your arms, elbows, and wrists into the floor. Rock gently from side to side, drawing your shoulders under your body to relieve pressure on your neck. Lengthen your spine by using your leg muscles to pull your thighs and hips higher.

3. Unclasping your hands, bend your arms at your elbows and place your hands on your back as far up your spine as you can, with fingers facing up toward the ceiling. Use your hands to support your back, bracing your elbows against the floor. Raise your legs up, one at a time, keeping a bend at the hips to help keep the pressure on your shoulders and off your neck.

4. Extend energy up through your legs, pressing your ankles together, spreading your toes, and pressing the balls of your feet up toward the ceiling. Breathe steadily and calmly. Hold for one to three minutes.

If you have your period or need to avoid putting strain on your neck, perform the Half Shoulderstand, as follows:

1. Place a bolster lengthwise about a foot from a wall. To get into position, sit on the bolster with your left side toward the wall. Begin to lie back, and pivot your lower body toward the wall, extending your legs upward. Use your hands to provide support as you do this.

2. Lie down perpendicular to the wall, with your lower back and hips on the bolster and your legs extending up the wall, ankles together. Rest your palms on your belly, at your sides facing up, or on the floor over your head in the shape of a diamond, with your elbows bent and fingertips touching. Hold this pose for two to ten minutes.

Benefits: Strengthens and calms the nervous system and emotions by stimulating the thyroid and parathyroid glands; deeply relaxing; excellent pose for overcoming insomnia.

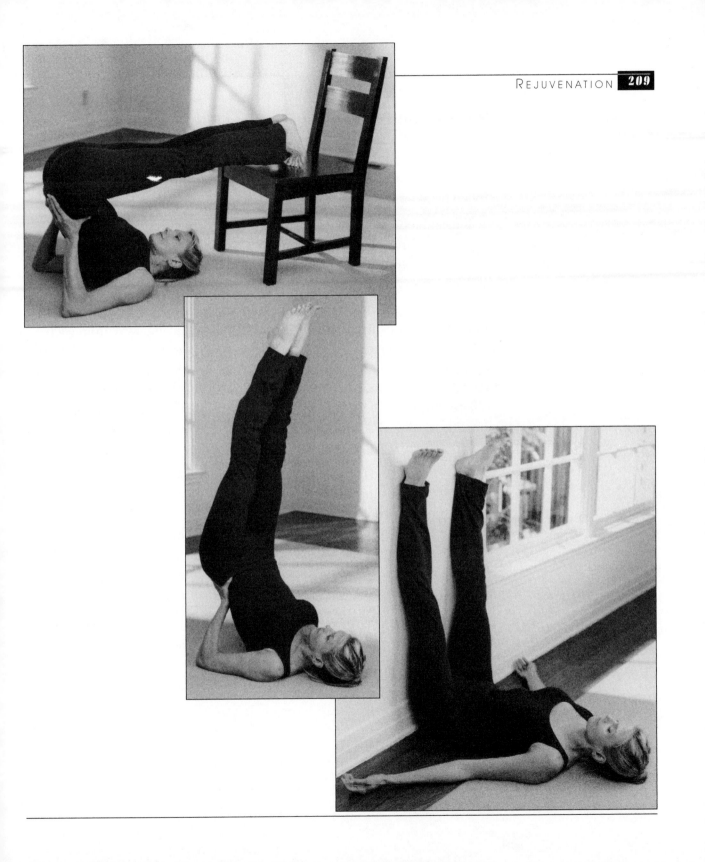

Relaxation Pose

1. Lie on your back with your legs comfortably apart and your arms by your sides, palms up. If you feel discomfort in your lower back, place a rolled blanket or bolster under your knees. Close your eyes.

2. Inhale deeply, hold your breath for a few seconds, and then exhale. Do this two or three more times. With each inhale, imagine that you're drawing up any tension in your body, and releasing it as you exhale. Lie completely still, allowing your breath to flow in and out effortlessly.

3. Let your eyes rest lightly closed, cultivating a sense of gazing inside. Relax your forehead and imagine your eyebrows falling away from each other, creating a feeling of calm between your eyes. Consciously relax your upper lip and feel all of the muscles in your face releasing tension, letting go. With your lips resting lightly closed, relax your tongue onto your palate and allow your jaw to release. With each exhale, feel your shoulders, ribs, hips, and legs sink more deeply into the floor.

4. Lying completely still, bring your attention to the feelings and sensations within your body. As your breath flows out, let all thoughts and images slip away. Notice your mind becoming quieter and more peaceful. Soften your neck, throat, and shoulders. Feel the rise and fall of your chest and belly, allowing your thighs to soften and roll effortlessly out to the sides. Let your legs, feet, and toes relax more deeply. Imagine that your bones are detaching from your muscles, sinking more and more into a complete state of relaxation and blissful calm. Lie for five to fifteen minutes.

Benefits: Relaxes, refreshes, rejuvenates; brings the body, mind, and spirit into balance; relieves tension and induces calmness of mind. Excellent for dealing with insomnia and releasing anxiety.

Chapter 11

Nutrition

The classic principles of healthy eating apply at menopause, just as much as ever. In fact, we have more reasons than ever to follow them. Think about it:

- We're still concerned about cutting fats and calories to bring our weight down, but we're further motivated to do so by the very real threat of heart disease.
- Lots of fresh fruits and vegetables are still smart choices for keeping our diet clean and our bodies lean. But getting the recommended five to eight servings a day also provides us with antioxidants and other plant substances that are so important for reducing cancer risk and protecting the arteries from plaque buildup.
- Resisting the quick fix of refined starches and sugary treats is still a safe bet for keeping blood sugar stable. During perimenopause, this has the added bonus of maintaining high energy levels and preventing mood swings.

Healthy eating will help keep your skin looking young, keep your thinking clear, and improve the quality of your sleep. In addition, specific foods can help balance hormones and reduce hormonal symptoms, like menstrual irregularities and hot flashes. In the long run, how we eat today influences our level of vitality and function in the many years to come.

Let's look at seven basic principles of healthy eating at midlife.

1. Calcium & Co.

Did you get your calcium today? If you did, good for you. But calcium is only one of the minerals our bones need. In fact, without the right additional minerals, little of the calcium we consume can be used. At least three of the "bone-health" minerals are needed in quantities that may be difficult to obtain from diet alone.

Calcium

Although many of us are aware of the need for calcium, we still don't get enough. Women need between 1,000 and 1,500 milligrams per day, depending on their age and degree of risk for bone loss.

Before age 50	1,000 mg
Age 50–65 (with HRT)	1,000 mg
Age 50–65 (no HRT)	1,500 mg
Over age 65	1,500 mg
Source: National Institute of Health	

Some good food sources of calcium are:

Nonfat or low-fat milk	8 oz.	300 mg
Yogurt	8 oz.	290 mg
Cheddar cheese	1 oz.	205 mg
Tofu	4 oz.	145 mg
Broccoli, cooked	8 oz.	130 mg

Other good sources of calcium include some green vegetables (such as kale, turnip greens, Chinese cabbage), some legumes, canned sardines, seeds, nuts, and certain fortified food products. Realistically, however, you're not likely to get all the calcium you need in your food, so you may need to take a supplement as well. Calcium carbonate is the most popular kind, although calcium citrate is more easily digested and is a better choice for older women.

Calcium Tips

• Stop smoking, and limit consumption of animal protein, salt, phosphorus (usually found in carbonated sodas), and caffeine—all these can rob your body of calcium.

• Calcium is best absorbed if you take it in doses of 500 milligrams or less, between meals. Avoid taking calcium with iron.

• To make sure your supplement will be easily digested, drop one tablet into a few ounces of vinegar. The tablet should dissolve within thirty minutes—if it doesn't, try another brand.

Magnesium and Vitamin D

A variety of other vitamins and minerals get into the bone-building act. Magnesium is especially important, and must be present in at least a 1:2 ratio to calcium. Whole grains, nuts, and beans are good sources of magnesium; if you're supplementing higher doses of calcium (to meet the 1,500-milligram recommendation), however, you'll probably need to take a magnesium supplement as well. Many calcium pills contain magnesium in the correct ratio.

Vitamin D, too, is a must-have for calcium absorption. Our bodies naturally manufacture vitamin D when our skin is exposed to sunlight. Unfortunately, prolonged sun exposure ages the skin and increases the risk of skin cancer. That's why it's important to supplement your sun exposure by consuming milk and other vitamin-D-enriched products, and taking 400 to 800 IU of vitamin D in pill form.

2. Phytoestrogens and Soy

There's a whole new food category to be aware of at midlife—
phytoestrogens.

Phytoestrogens are plant substances that have a mild *estrogenic* effect on the body. Soy, for example, contains chemical compounds called isoflavones, which can bind with estrogen receptors in the body. Because they're much weaker than your natural estrogen, they can serve in two ways. First, if you're low on estrogen, isoflavones in soy may provide just enough to relieve some of the symptoms.

Frequently, though, women in perimenopause—whose estrogen levels may be fluctuating dramatically—are experiencing the effects of too *much* estrogen. Such effects can include heavy bleeding and higher risk of developing breast cancer. In this situation, weak estrogen from plant sources helps by preventing your body's own estrogen from attaching to estrogen receptors. By replacing a stronger estrogen with a weaker one, phytoestrogens help balance hormone levels and relieve the symptoms of hormonal fluctuation. This can mean less bleeding, and less risk of developing perimenopausal breast cancer.

Isoflavones from soy protein have been shown to reduce hot flashes by as much as 45 percent and to protect the heart by lowering levels of LDL cholesterol by as much as 13 percent, according to a 1995 analysis of studies. In addition, soy may also help prevent bone loss. In a recent study at the University of Illinois, postmenopausal women who took 40 grams of soy protein powder per day (containing 90 milligrams of isoflavones) increased their spinal bone density while significantly improving blood cholesterol levels as well.

Experts recommend eating about one or two servings of soy per day, containing about 40 to 80 milligrams of isoflavones. Typical servings would be a cup of edamame, a glass of soy milk, or a couple of ounces of tofu. It's important to note the isoflavone content of the soy food you choose, because this can vary widely—whole soybeans, for instance, contain about ten times the isoflavones as soy hot dogs or soy yogurt.

Too Much of a Good Thing?

Because soy protein does have an estrogenlike effect, some health practicioners worry that eating too much of it—especially after menopause—could pose the same cancer risks as long-term estrogen replacement therapy. According to Dr. Mary Hardy, however—a botanical medicine specialist and head of the Integrative Medical Group of Cedars Sinai Medical Center in Los Angeles—there is no evidence of danger when soy is obtained from food sources.

Hardy notes that women in Asia, who eat a soy-rich diet, do not show a corresponding increased incidence of cancer. In fact, Japanese and Chinese studies reported last year in *Health Magazine* found that women who consumed more soy had a significantly *lower* risk of breast cancer than those who ate the least. Stick to one to two servings from food sources, she says, and you're unlikely to overdo it.

The danger from taking soy in concentrated supplement form is that you can quickly run up into dosages that have not been evaluated for safety in humans. If you do use a soy protein powder or supplement, keep your intake below 80 to 100 milligrams of isoflavones a day. Also, be advised that, as with peanuts, allergic reactions to soy can occur.

Good Food Sources of Isoflavones

Soy Products
- Raw soybeans
- Soy flour
- Miso soup
- Tempeh (pressed fermented soybean cake, similar to tofu but stronger in taste)
- Soy cheese
- Tofu
- Soy milk (pureed soybeans and water; available in flavors and regular, low-fat, and nonfat versions; a 1-cup serving has 130 calories, 4 grams of fat, no cholesterol, and 10 grams of protein)

- Soy protein concentrate
- Soy protein isolate (an almost tasteless white powder containing approximately 90 percent protein; it's the most refined form of soy protein, and is available in flavors)

Other Sources of Phytoestrogens
- Flaxseed oil
- Sunflower seeds
- Red clover
- Bean sprouts
- Green beans
- Brown rice
- Radishes
- Potatoes
- Bioflavinoids found in berries and the peels of citrus fruits may also help hot flashes

3. Choose Fats You Can Live With

It's probably not news that limiting the fat you eat is vital for heart health and keeping your weight down. But not all fat is bad fat. While the American Heart Association recommends limiting total fat intake to 30 percent or less of your calories, new research shows that the *type* of fat you eat may be even more important than the amount.

Generally cutting back on fats will lower your overall cholesterol level. The fats in your bloodstream, however, include both "bad" LDLs and "good" HDLs. Any across-the-board cut in dietary fat is likely to reduce the good along with the bad. The better move is to not only decrease your total fat intake but also minimize your calories from *saturated fat,* in favor of fats that have more beneficial effects on the body.

It's important to get to know your fats so you can be more selective about which you choose. Don't be too discouraged by the first few in this list; the news gets better as you read on.

Saturated Fats

Saturated fats, mainly from animal sources, can be lethal. They choke the arteries, raising blood cholesterol; in so doing, they contribute more to heart disease than any other fats. Most saturated fats are solid at room temperature, but there are exceptions. Tropical vegetable oils (palm and coconut), though liquid, are also highly saturated. And even though I know you're not buying these by the bottle, beware: They're used in hundreds of processed foods, from chips and cookies to so-called healthy energy bars. Although meat and dairy are good sources of protein and other nutrients, it's best to limit your saturated fat consumption to no more than 7 to 10 percent of your total calories.

Recommendation

Minimize your intake by choosing lower-fat cuts of beef, removing skin from chicken, eating fish two to three times per week as your protein source, and replacing the animal protein in your diet with soy protein as much as possible.

Transfatty Acids

In some ways, these are the worst of the worst because, unlike saturated fat from animal sources, they often turn up in foods of little nutritional value. Transfats are found in margarine and shortening, are used in the frying vats of fast-food restaurants, and show up in numerous processed foods. Through a process called hydrogenation, these fats are given a longer shelf life—while at the same time increasing your risk of heart attack. Data from the Nurses Health Study showed a 50 percent greater risk of heart attack in women who consumed transfats than those who didn't. Look for "partially hydrogenated vegetable oils" on the label, and steer clear.

Recommendation

Minimize or eliminate transfat by avoiding fried foods, and processed foods containing partially hydrogenated vegetable oils.

Polyunsaturated Fats

This group includes most vegetable oils (other than palm and coconut oils). While less dangerous than saturated fats, polyunsaturated fats may cause problems by lowering levels of "good" cholesterol.

Recommendation

The less, the better. When possible, replace with monounsaturated oils.

Monounsaturated Fats

Researchers have searched for a reason why folks in Mediterranean countries have only about half the rate of heart attacks we do. While other factors undoubtedly contribute, studies show that monounsaturated oils, especially olive oil, can lower LDLs in your blood and make them less susceptible to oxidation from free radicals.

Recommendation

Good choice for cooking whenever appropriate. Along with omega-3 sources, monounsaturated oils should make up as much of your total fat consumption as possible.

Essential Fatty Acids (Omega-3 and Omega-6)

Omega-3 and omega-6 are two families of essential fatty acids (EFAs) your body relies on for normal cell function and hormone production. Most of us already get more than enough omega-6s, which are mostly polyunsaturated fats. Omega-3 fatty acids, contained in many fish oils, are associated with a wide range of health benefits including lowering blood pressure and cholesterol, and reducing clotting. Omega-3s may also help protect against breast cancer. Various types of fish—including salmon, tuna, sardines, herring, cod, and others—are great sources of omega-3s. Another good choice is flaxseed oil. *Tip:* Flaxseed oil must be kept fresh to be effective. Store small quantities of the oil in the refrigerator, or purchase flaxseeds and grind them a coffee grinder as needed. Ground seeds are a nice addition to cereal or blended fruit drinks.

Recommendation

The most efficient way to get the necessary amount of EFAs in your diet is to consume two to three servings of fish a week or 1 to 2 teaspoons of fresh-ground flaxseed per day.

Fats at a Glance

- Keep your fat consumption under 25 percent of your total calories for the day, with as much as possible supplied by monounsaturated oils and foods containing essential fatty acids.
- Limit saturated fats (animal and dairy fats) to 7 to 10 percent of your total calories.
- Eat two to three servings of fish per week, or some other source of omega-3 fatty acids, such as flaxseed oil, or a supplement.

ESSENTIAL Omega-3s	BEST FATS FOR COOKING Monounsaturated	MINIMIZE Polyunsaturated	LIMIT/MODIFY (GOOD PROTEIN SOURCES WHEN FAT CONTENT IS KEPT LOW)	AVOID Transfatty Acids
• Salmon	• Olive oil	• Safflower oil	**Saturated**	• Baked goods
• Tuna	• Canola oil	• Sesame oil	• Meats	• Fried foods
• Other fish	• Peanut oil	• Soy oil	• Dairy	• Snack foods
• Flaxseed oil		• Corn oil		• Most margarine
• Canola oil		• Sunflower oil		• Fast foods
• Walnuts		• Nuts		• Processed frozen meals
• Green vegetables		• Seeds		**Saturated Fats**
				• Palm oil
				• Coconut oil

4. Easy Does It: Sugar, Caffeine, and Salt

You probably already know about the importance of limiting your intake of sugar, caffeine, and salt, but the need is even greater when you're on that hormonal trampoline preceding menopause. Cutting back on these much-overdone dietary crutches will help you avoid mood swings, weight gain, insomnia—as well as long-term threats like hypertension and bone loss.

Refined Sweets: 10 Percent or Less of Total Calories

Refined sugar is a quick fix. And for those desperate midafternoon can't-get-my-work-done moments, it's very tempting. But if you're like me, your sugar buzz soon turns into a crash. That crash, in turn, may cause you to overeat, to compensate for the drop in blood sugar. This pattern of *rush, crash,* and *binge* can have terrible effects on your mood and your waist-line. In addition, a high sugar intake encourages calcium to be excreted in the urine, sucking the minerals from your bones.

One of my strategies is to never eat anything really sugary on an empty stomach. Not only does this cause me to eat less, but what I do eat doesn't affect my blood sugar level so drastically, and therefore doesn't affect my energy and mood as much.

- No more than 10 percent of total calories from any sweetened foods.
- Avoid sugar on an empty stomach.
- When you feel the urge to eat refined sweets, try a natural whole-food source of sugar like a piece of fruit first to see if that might satisfy the craving.

Never Say Never

There are times, I know, when that piece of chocolate cake won't be denied. That's fine: Save the chocolate for only those times and I bet you'll end up eating a lot less of it. There really are no bad foods, there are just bad habits *involving* food. If, instead of making certain foods "illegal," you reserve them for when you feel you really *must* have them, it saves you from feeling deprived and frees you to make healthy choices more of the time. The way to change a bad habit is to focus on developing good habits.

Caffeine: Three Beverages or Less

For those who enjoy it, a small amount of caffeine provides a pleasant lift; it revs you up and increases your ability to concentrate. As people get older, though, they often become more caffeine sensitive. Drinking too much can cause jittery nerves, sleeplessness, and heart palpitations. Because caffeine is a diuretic, it may contribute to dehydration, affecting skin tone and vaginal lubrication. Caffeine can also trigger hot flashes. If you're trying to limit your intake, be aware of hidden sources such as sodas, chocolate, and various cold medications.

- Don't drink caffeine within six hours of going to sleep.
- Notice whether your caffeine intake may be causing hot flashes.
- Drink at least one extra glass of water for every caffeinated beverage you drink.
- Experiment with lower-octane sources of caffeine, such as green tea. Green tea contains only a third of the caffeine in coffee and may have anticancer properties as well.

Salt: 2,400 Milligrams a Day or Less

Researchers at the Northwestern School of Medicine tested subjects with high blood pressure using a low-fat diet and three different levels of sodium. They found that the lower sodium fell, the lower blood pressure went, too. Subjects who ate a very low level of sodium—1,500 milligrams a day— got twice the benefit over those who merely ate a low-fat diet.

Simply minimizing your reliance on processed and restaurant food can cut your salt intake by up to 75 percent. As much as possible, steer away from heavily salted foods such as salt-cured and smoked meats, and limit your consumption of frozen dinners, canned soups, and lunch meats. Restaurant dinners are the worst offenders, guaranteeing you at least 1,000 milligrams of sodium, and possibly much more, depending on what you order. Cheese fries with ranch dressing? That's 5,000 milligrams—more than the test subjects in the Northwestern study mentioned above ate in three days! For best results, try to keep your sodium intake under 2,400 milligrams per day.

5. Optimize Your Energy Nutrients

We're lucky to live in a country where food is plentiful. This *should* make it easier to make healthy choices. But when the supermarket aisles are crowded with hot dogs, cheese dips, ice cream, and frozen pizza, it's easy to lose sight of one of the most basic principles of healthful eating, which is, as much as possible, to eat fresh, whole foods.

I'm a big believer in maximizing the power of the major nutrients—protein, carbohydrate, and fat—by consuming a diet rich in fresh produce and unrefined grains. If you do this, you'll get a balanced complement of vitamins, minerals, and fiber, you'll be eating fewer calories, and you'll naturally be consuming less fat, salt, and chemical preservatives.

Experts differ on the optimum percentages of the major nutrients. I've always favored a moderate approach, which I find keeps me feeling satisfied while giving me plenty of energy to get through my workouts:

Protein	20–25%
Carbohydrates	55–60%
Fats	20–25%

Despite the current trend toward high-protein diets, large amounts of protein can add extra saturated fat to your diet and create waste products that put unnecessary strain on the kidneys.

Two of the major benefits of eating more whole foods are more fiber, and a greater assortment of micronutrients.

More Fiber

More fiber in a meal helps you feel full sooner, making it less likely you'll overeat. Fiber also acts as a natural laxative. Soluble fiber—available in apples and other fruits, beans, oats, bran, and carrots—lowers your cholesterol, reducing the chance of heart disease. Your body will thank you if you consume about 13 grams for every 1,000 calories. Since most people eat only about 10 grams, you're likely to notice a real difference in how you feel.

Vitamins and Minerals

If carbohydrate, protein, and fat are the fuel that makes your body run, vitamins and minerals are the "tune-up" that makes it run most efficiently. These micronutrients perform a vast number of functions related to general health and vitality. Many of them offer additional benefits at midlife as well. *Vitamin E*, for example, protects your heart and may relieve hot flashes and vaginal dryness. *Vitamin C* gives your adrenals a boost, which will help with fatigue and may boost bone mineral density. In a study in the *Journal of Bone and Mineral Research*, researchers concluded that vitamin C appeared to enhance the effects of estrogen therapy and calcium supplements. Women who took 1,000 milligrams or more of the *vitamin C* had higher levels of bone density than those who took less. The *B vitamins* are the real stress busters: 500 to 1,000 milligrams of B_6 a day will improve sleep and lift mood. B complex and *vitamin A* are important for dry skin and hair. Eating fresh whole foods guarantees you not only greater quantities of these vitamins, but also a variety of other beneficial compounds present in plant foods, such as phytohormones.

Here are some general guidelines:

- **Eat more fresh fruits and vegetables.** The average American eats less then two servings of fruits and vegetables a day. Try to get at least three servings of vegetables and two servings of fruits each day—and preferably more.
- **Eat more whole grains.** Refined grains are often devoid of beneficial fiber. Look for products that contain 100 percent whole grain.
- **Eat more green leafy vegetables.** Vegetables such as spinach, chard, and kale are rich with vital nutrients—especially calcium and magnesium for stronger bones. Consuming more than two daily servings of dark green and deep yellow vegetables has been shown to decrease risk for heart disease by nearly 50 percent.
- **Choose foods in their least processed form.** Choose an apple instead of apple juice, brown rice over white rice, and fresh turkey over processed lunch meats.

Breakfast Sets the Tone

Every morning here in Los Angeles, the highways are crawling with women munching down breakfast bars and coffee-to-go. I lead as busy a life as anyone, but I still say breakfast deserves more thought.

Here's how I've started every day for the last fifteen years. I walk downstairs, start a pot of water boiling, and throw in steel-cut oats or another whole-grain cereal. While it's cooking, I make my kids' lunch and vegetable snacks for the day. When my cereal is ready, I add sliced bananas and strawberries. Finally, I pour on soy milk and sprinkle on walnuts and ground flaxseed. What a combination! You've got sweetness from the fruit, a little fat from milk, B vitamins, omega-3s, phytoestrogens—all in about 450 calories. How can you overeat when you're eating this thick, chewy, soul-satisfying cereal? Add a couple of glasses of water and you're full.

If you start the day with a healthy meal, you're more likely to eat healthy the rest of the day. Eating whole grains like this sets a great example for my kids, too. When my girls go to a friend's house and someone serves them white bread, they tell me it doesn't even taste like bread to them. Makes me proud!

Variety

There's no one perfect food to eat all the time. Most people have a short list of favorite foods, which is fine, but it's good to rotate in some others. One very simple way to get a greater range of nutrients in your diet is by *color*. Plants evolved in a rich array of colors to protect them from the destructive effects of the environment. The same chemicals that give plants their color, protect us against disease and premature aging. Each color provides a different combination of micronutrients that, together, provide a buffer from the harmful effects of sunlight and oxidation. That's why variety is key. Create a spectrum of fruits and vegetables in your diet, including some from each of the following color categories: red, orange, light and dark green, white, and purple.

6. Water

Imagine a garden that's not getting enough water. It could scarcely thrive, and might not survive at all. Water is just as vital to our bodies, and the effects of dehydration are just as damaging. Drinking plenty of water is especially important in midlife, for keeping skin tone beautiful and vaginal tissue moist. It also helps keep your kidneys functioning properly and flushes bacteria from the bladder to prevent infection.

Often, people think they're hungry when really they're just thirsty. Drinking a glass of water before each meal can help curb your appetite and keep you well hydrated at the same time. To calculate your water needs, divide your weight by three. This is the number of ounces you should be getting every day. Add another 8 ounces for each hour of exercise and for every caffeinated or alcoholic drink you consume.

7. Good Eating Habits

Keep a Food Diary

It's amazing how in denial some people are about what they put into their bodies! That's why I always recommend keeping a food diary for a week whenever you're setting out to modify your diet. Aside from giving you a gauge of your total calories, balance of nutrients, ratio of whole foods to processed foods, number of sugary snacks, and so on, your diary can also help you associate your eating patterns with perimenopausal symptoms of moods, sleep problems, and hot flashes. No matter how in touch you think you are with your eating, I guarantee that the diary will reveal some surprises and provide added incentive to make positive changes.

Eat More Often

Eating four or five smaller meals throughout the day will help keep your blood sugar levels from plunging and spiking. This will give you more energy throughout the day and help to stabilize your mood.

Calorie Deficit—Gotta *Burn* It to *Earn* It

One of the worst things about menopause for many women is weight gain. It's not just an appearance issue, either; even 10 extra pounds can increase the risk of developing osteoarthritis of the knees, not to mention the strain it puts on the heart and other organs. Part of the problem is hormonal. Changes in hormone levels can cause you to retain water—in essence creating weight gain. At the same time, hormonal changes may affect the distribution of fat. You may actually weigh the same, but the fat may have migrated to places where you *really* don't want it, like around your waist.

Much of the problem, though, is that we literally have more *years* under our belts, years in which we probably haven't been exercising as much. Some amount of weight gain is almost inevitable without a strenuous effort at cutting back on the calories and increasing activity. All the nutritional guidelines in this chapter will support weight loss, but the final criteria is always that one simple question: Did you eat fewer calories than you burned? Remember: You gotta *burn* it to *earn* it!

Don't Excessively Restrict Calories

It's probably not wise for most active women to eat fewer than 1,500 calories a day—even when trying to lose weight. So many factors determine your real metabolic needs that no basic food plan can satisfy everyone perfectly. That's why you should base your own calorie intake on your level of hunger. The key is to stop when you've had enough. When you're eating the right proportion of nutrients, you'll find you'll be more satisfied and better able to determine your caloric needs by your hunger level.

Meal Planning and Preparation

If you're deciding what you're going to eat at six at night when you're headed home, it's a recipe for disaster. I recommend planning your meals at the beginning of the week, and then doing your shopping with your plan in mind. That way, you can avoid the impulse buying that ultimately leads to impulse eating.

Second, take advantage of the fact that willpower is strongest in the morning. If you make all the preparations for a healthy day's eating when you first wake up, you're very likely to eat well that day. Not only do I often prepare my lunch in the morning, but I also cut up a selection of fruits and vegetables that I can snack on through the day. I've found that when I make healthy eating easy for myself, I'm far less likely to go looking for some sugary, fat-laden treat.

Portion Sizes

Many people are familiar with the Food Pyramid, a simple visual device for assembling nutritionally balanced meals. In the Food Pyramid, plant foods are the basis of your daily intake. For a woman consuming about 1,600 calories a day, six servings should come from grains, five from fruits and vegetables, and only two each from the dairy and meat groups.

But here's the catch: In our effort to restrict excess calories while maintaining proper nutrition, what's often missing is a good, solid definition of the word *serving*. To some people, it's whatever quantity they can eat at one sitting. Absurd as that sounds, I think we've all been guilty of it. We assume that one serving equals however many chips are in the bag, or whatever amount of potatoes the restaurant serves. But that's not how it works!

The U.S. Department of Agriculture sets guidelines for the portion sizes in the Food Pyramid. The tricky thing is, official servings may not coincide with what we think of as traditional portions. For example, a single slice of bread, according to USDA guidelines, is one serving. This means that when you eat a sandwich, you're consuming *two* servings from the grain category. Depending on your calorie goal, this may constitute as much as one third of your grain quota for the day!

In fact, let's take a closer look at that sandwich. Add a few ounces of tuna or turkey and a couple of slices of cheese, and it now contains about half your daily quota for protein and dairy. It adds up fast! To learn more about the Food Pyramid and serving sizes, you can access the Department of Agriculture's Web site at www.usda.gov. Here are some sample serving sizes, taken from the USDA's *Dietary Guidelines for Americans,* fifth edition:

> **HEALTHY SNACKS**
> - Baked apples with walnuts and raisins with a little orange juice sprinkled on top (bake in a toaster oven)
> - Pineapple cottage cheese with Grape-nuts sprinkled on top
> - Peanut or cashew butter spread on apple slices or celery
> - Sliced bell peppers of all colors or sliced jicama

PORTION SIZES

Grain—6 Servings
- 1 slice of bread
- 1 cup of dry cereal
- $1/2$ cup of cooked cereal, rice, or pasta

Vegetables—3 Servings
- 1 cup of raw leafy vegetables
- $1/2$ cup of other vegetables, cooked or raw

Fruit—2 Servings
- 1 medium apple, banana, orange, or pear
- $1/2$ cup chopped, cooked, or canned fruit
- $3/4$ cup of fruit juice

Dairy—2 Servings (children 9–18 and women over 50 should have 3 servings)
- 1 cup of low-fat milk or yogurt
- $1^{1}/2$ ounces of natural cheese

Protein—2 Servings
- 2–3 ounces of cooked lean meat, poultry, or fish
- 1 cup of cooked beans or tofu (counts as one serving of protein)
- 5-ounce soy burger
- 2–3 eggs
- 4 tablespoons peanut butter

Source: USDA

The first few times you prepare meals according to these guidelines, it may seem restrictive. You may not be used to seeing large amounts of vegetables and grains on your plate alongside small servings of meat. In fact, you may not be used to seeing vegetables at all! But you'll be surprised what a difference this simple framework can make. You'll discover how easy it is to prepare healthy, low-fat meals without counting every calorie.

Moving Through Menopause Nutritional Checklist

- Reduce consumption of fast food and processed foods.
- Focus on fresh fruits and vegetables, low-fat proteins, and whole grains.
- Keep saturated fat consumption between 7 and 10 percent of your daily calories, and total fat between 25 and 30 percent.
- Keep protein intake under 25 percent of total calories.
- Limit refined sugar, caffeine, and salt.
- Eat 25 to 40 grams of soy per day, containing 40 to 80 milligrams of isoflavones.
- Eat two to three servings a week of fish or some other source of omega-3 fatty acids.
- Make sure you get 13 grams of fiber for every 1,000 calories.
- Drink approximately six to eight glasses of water a day, depending on your weight and activity.
- Eat four to five smaller meals every day.
- Take daily multivitamin/mineral supplements providing the following:
  - Calcium, 1,000 to 1,500 milligrams, depending on age and risk factors
  - Vitamin D, 400 to 800 IU
  - Magnesium, 500 to 750 milligrams, depending on calcium intake
  - Bioflavinoids, 1,500 milligrams per day in divided doses
  - Vitamin E, 400 to 800 IU
  - Vitamin C, 500 to 2,000 milligrams, in divided doses
  - B complex, 25 to 50 milligrams
  - B_6, 500 to 1,000 milligrams, in divided doses
  - Vitamin A, 5,000 milligrams, in divided doses

Chapter 12

HRT

Although we've been mainly focused on lifestyle factors, no book about menopause would be complete without a discussion of hormone replacement therapy. Twenty million Americans now take either ERT (estrogen alone) or HRT (a combination of hormones). They do it for two main reasons: to relieve perimenopausal and menopausal symptoms, and to lower their risk of developing osteoporosis and heart disease.

Because ERT and HRT can banish debilitating symptoms, many of my friends have found them to be a godsend. On the other hand, hormone replacement is not an exact science—yet. Women's bodies are all very different; a level of estrogen that's normal for one might feel horrible to another. Some of my other friends have had trouble finding medication that didn't leave them feeling worse than the symptoms they were trying to treat.

Add to this the fact that *long-term* benefits and risks are still not fully known. Every week, it seems, new study results make the headlines. It's difficult even for the medical professional to sort through them—let alone the rest of us.

Nevertheless, especially in the area of long-term health, the stakes are potentially high, and a woman owes it to herself to make an informed decision. I've tried to help by outlining the essential information that will enable you to have a more in-depth conversation with your doctor. I've been aided immensely in preparing this chapter by Prudence Hall, M.D., Dan Cosgrove, M.D., and my own doctor, Paula Bernstein, M.D.

The Big Decision

Deciding about HRT requires looking not only at your physical situation but also your attitudes about medication. Some women are fiercely opposed to taking synthetic hormones and feel tremendous shame and guilt when the severity of their symptoms leaves them no choice. Other women battle symptoms for months or years before "giving in" to HRT, only to sigh with relief: "It's the best thing I ever did—why did I wait so long?"

So far, I've been able to maintain a high level of well-being through exercise, nutrition, and other lifestyle factors alone. But I'm keeping an open mind about the potential long-term health benefits of HRT. Since I'm still having periods, I'm not forced to make an immediate decision, but I plan to stay on top of new evidence as it becomes available so I'll be ready to decide when the time comes.

Two important points:

- If you do decide to begin HRT, be sure to also follow the exercise and dietary recommendations in this book. Not only is this important from the standpoint of overall health, but studies have shown that women who take estrogen and exercise regularly experience greater increases in bone density than those who take HRT without exercising.
- Even if you decide *against* taking hormones, it's still important to maintain a relationship with your doctor. He or she can monitor your general health and symptoms and help you assess how your lifestyle changes or alternative therapies are working.

When to Seek Professional Help

In addition to regular checkups, you should see your doctor if you have any of the following:

- Heavy bleeding
- Unbearable symptoms
- Long-term health concerns (degenerative disease or family history)
- If you feel like you're experiencing an emotional crisis

A Range of Choices

There are many types of hormone replacement therapy involving estrogen and progesterone, either separately or in combination. Sometimes testosterone is prescribed as well. Some formulas give you a monthly period, others don't. Hormone therapy is available in many forms, including pills, patches, creams, drops, and injections. Some formulas are aimed at improving symptoms; some are designed only to strengthen your bones and heart; still others do both. The choice of hormone will depend on your needs, but finding just the right formula and dose for your body can be a trial-and-error process.

Benefits of Hormone Replacement Therapy

Hormone replacement can usually help tremendously with symptoms. It's important to understand, however, that the long-term benefits and risks are still being studied and debated. Nevertheless, most experts agree the current evidence supports the following benefits:

- ### _Relief from Symptoms_
  Estrogen replacement therapy will generally relieve hot flashes and vaginal dryness, and can help with depression, irritability, and sleep

problems. It may also decrease incontinence by improving tone in the urethra and pelvic muscles (although you should keep doing your Kegels). Some women find that estrogen moisturizes and plumps up the skin, smoothing out fine wrinkles.

• _Stronger Bones and Protection Against Osteoporosis_

Estrogen therapy is considered by many to be the most effective treatment for osteoporosis and the best way to rein in the sudden bone loss after menopause. A woman on estrogen can reduce her risk of hip fracture by 50 percent and spinal fractures by 90 percent. Some experts believe the best time to get this benefit is in the five to ten years immediately after menopause, when bone loss is at its height. Protection lasts only as long as you continue taking the hormone; to get the full benefit, you need to stay on HRT until the rate of bone loss slows down naturally, some time around age sixty-five.

• _Protection Against Heart Disease_

Estrogen appears to raise "good" HDLs while lowering "bad" LDLs, possibly reducing the risk of atherosclerosis. Estrogen also dilates the coronary arteries, improving blood flow to the heart. Some studies have concluded that ERT lowers the risk of heart attack in healthy post-menopausal women by 50 percent, but more research is under way to test these benefits. Because of the high risk of heart disease after menopause, these heart-friendly effects constitute one of the greatest potential benefits of ERT; the effects may not be as great when progesterone is added, however —and progesterone is recommended, except in women who've had a hysterectomy.

• _Possible Improved Memory and Delay of Onset of Alzheimer's Disease_

Early data suggest that Alzheimer's, if it occurs, may develop later and progress more slowly in women on ERT. In one study, scientists following women at Leisure World over an eleven-year period found that the risk of Alzheimer's disease and related dementia was less in estrogen users than in nonusers. Although estrogen doesn't appear to be effective at _reversing_ cognitive decline or dementia, it may, with more study, turn out to play an important role in prevention.

Risks of Hormone Replacement Therapy

• _Uterine Cancer_

Taking estrogen alone for longer than about five years raises the risk for uterine (endometrial) cancer by as much as 300 percent in women who still have a uterus. Using HRT preparations that include progesterone eliminates this risk.

• _Breast Cancer_

This is a controversial area. While ERT advocates claim that most studies have _not_ shown higher risks of breast cancer in women who take estrogens, opponents cite studies showing that _long-term use_ (five to fifteen years) may increase the normal risk of breast cancer by 30 to 40 percent. Nevertheless, because the _absolute_ lifetime risk of breast cancer is so low to start with, this only raises it from about 10 percent to about 14 percent. Many women, concerned with the much greater danger of heart disease, view this as an acceptable risk in exchange for the potential benefits of estrogen, as long as they don't have any additional risk factors for breast cancer. It's definitely something to discuss with your doctor.

• _Gallbladder Disease_

Women on oral estrogen have a higher incidence of gallstones and other gallbladder disease. This risk can be avoided by using an estrogen patch.

Side Effects

The most common side effects of HRT are sleepiness, migraines, bloating, and weight gain.

Don't be afraid to talk to your doctor about any side effects you experience. I recommend keeping a journal of your symptoms, and returning in a month to discuss the possibility of adjusting your hormones to eliminate some of those symptoms. Your doctor can either switch you to a different type of hormone or lower the dose. In some cases, balancing the estrogen with natural progesterone can help.

Estrogens

Walking in to your doctor's office, you're most likely to get a synthetic hormone called Premarin, which—as no one ever forgets once they hear it—is made from *pregnant mare*'s ur*ine*. It's the most widely available estrogen today. Because most of the studies done on ERT are done with Premarin, more is known about its potential risks and benefits. *There are many other choices available, however.*

"Natural" Versus Synthetic

The term *natural* is a marketing buzzword. Pharmaceutical companies have latched on to it because, of course, women of our generation love anything "natural." The trouble is, there are no set criteria for what makes a hormone natural. A more meaningful term is *bioidentical hormone,* which many doctors feel—and it makes sense to me—are the true natural hormones. *Bioidentical* means identical to those our body produces.

Although Premarin's conjugated (or "joined-together") horse estrogens are a *natural* product of horses, they're still not natural to our bodies, because they're not identical to human estrogens. The same is true of synthetic, conjugated estrogens made from soybeans and other plants. Before the body can use them, it must first convert them to another form.

Bioidentical and Compounded Estrogens

The bioidentical estrogens are *estriol, estradiol,* and *estrone*—they're the three types of estrogen our body produces. When a woman takes any of these hormones, her body can't tell them apart from what her own body makes. Some doctors believe this produces fewer side effects.

Bioidentical estrogens are generic and can't be patented, so you won't find the major pharmaceutical companies promoting them. Still, increasing numbers of physicians are using them to treat symptoms of perimenopause. Some of the most promising results seem to be obtained from the newer *compounded* estrogens. These are bioidentical estrogens—typically, a blend of estradiol, estriol, and estrone—custom-made to your doctor's specifications by a compounding pharmacy. They're available in creams, drops, or pills, and may be mixed with a bioidentical progesterone as well.

In addition, doctors are increasingly prescribing estradiol in a patch form. By transmitting the drug through the skin, the patch enables it to escape breakdown in the liver. The upside of this is that it allows you to take lower doses, while also reducing the risk of blood clots. The downside of the patch is that, in bypassing the liver, the estrogen has no opportunity to affect cholesterol synthesis there. So if your main motive is heart protection, you need the pill, not the patch.

Bioidentical hormones work well for controlling symptoms and are well tolerated because they are relatively gentle. Nevertheless, research suggests they convey the same potential heart and bone benefits as synthetic estrogens such as Premarin. In addition, bioidentical hormones may carry a lower cancer risk than the synthetics.

According to Daniel Cosgrove, M.D., of the WellMax Center in La Quinta, CA, many of the unwanted side effects of hormone replacement therapy can be avoided by following two simple principles:

- Use bioidentical hormones.
- Avoid oral hormones.

Again, your doctor will help you determine the best choice for you.

Estrogen and Endometrial Cancer

Why do some women take estrogen alone, and others take it in combination with progesterone? One important reason is the risk of endometrial cancer that exists for some women on ERT alone. Estrogen stimulates the lining of the uterus and makes it thicken. During the normal monthly cycle, your body's own progesterone limits this growth and eventually causes the lining to shed, giving you your period. But women who aren't ovulating don't produce progesterone. For them, taking estrogen may cause their uterine lining to grow unchecked, and this can lead to endometrial cancer. For postmenopausal women who still have a uterus, taking progesterone limits endometrial growth and protects them from possible cancer. Women who've had a hysterectomy can safely take estrogen alone.

Progesterone

Perimenopause is characterized by huge swings in our estrogen level—first it soars, then it crashes. It's not always the case that women don't have enough estrogen in perimenopause; sometimes they have too much. That's where progesterone can help.

Progesterone is an important complement to estrogen. It can be used several ways:

• In perimenopause, progesterone creams can help balance out the body's own hormones without the use of any estrogen at all.

• Progesterone may be included with ERT in postmenopausal women who still have a uterus, to prevent an elevated risk for endometrial cancer.

Progesterone, like estrogen, is available in synthetic and natural, or bioidentical, varieties. The synthetic progesterones, or *progestins,* are more common in this country. The one most often prescribed in the United States is called Provera. Some doctors, like Dr. Prudence Hall, are concerned that synthetic progestins may increase the risk of heart disease—or at least cancel out any heart benefits from ERT. In addition, she says, they can cause women to feel bloated, angry, and depressed. (Two newer progestins—norgestimate and norethindrone acetate—appear to have fewer side effects than Provera and a better effect on blood lipids.)

For these reasons, many doctors prefer the bioidentical progesterones. The bioidentical progesterones, Hall says, create a sense of well-being, with fewer side effects. Until recently, these were available only in cream form. Recently, however, an oral form called *micronized progesterone* has become available. Micronized progesterone—in which the progesterone is broken up into small pieces for better absorption—protects the uterus without blocking ERT's good effects on the heart. Even when used without estrogen, it appears to strengthen bone and relieve hot flashes.

Also available are over-the-counter progesterone creams, such as Progest and others. Like the prescription creams, these can be very helpful for balancing out the surges in a woman's natural estrogen during perimenopause. Unfortunately, though, over-the-counter creams are not considered strong enough to compensate for the increased risk of uterine cancer on ERT. A postmenopausal woman with a uterus who's taking ERT still needs some type of prescription progesterone or progestin.

Testosterone

While estrogen therapy does help restore vaginal tissue and make sex more comfortable, that's not always enough to resurrect a low libido. In this case, your doctor may prescribe testosterone.

Testosterone levels vary greatly in women, and doctors don't know what constitutes a normal amount for any one person. In supplementing testosterone, it's necessary to experiment with doses and preparations. Besides raising sexual interest, testosterone can provide relief from breast tenderness sometimes caused by HRT. Testosterone is available in combination with estrogen in pill form called Estratest. A patch is in development, awaiting FDA approval. Meanwhile, your doctor can have testosterone capsules or gel made to order at a compounding pharmacy.

I've watched the gleam come back into some of my friends' eyes after just a few weeks on supplemental testosterone. Nevertheless, be sure to discuss possible risks with your doctor. Long-term risks are not known. Negative side effects can include facial and chest hair, a deeper voice, acne, increased cholesterol, and enlargement of the clitoris—none of which sounds particularly sexy.

WHO SHOULD NOT TAKE ERT OR HRT

- Anyone pregnant, immediately after childbirth, or while breast-feeding
- Anyone experiencing unusual vaginal bleeding that hasn't been checked by a physician
- Anyone who's had breast or uterine (endometrial) cancer
- Anyone with a history of blood clots

Weighing the Options

Step 1. Consider Your Symptoms

Obviously, if you're having to change the sheets three times a night because of your hot flashes, your symptoms certainly warrant treatment. But what if, like me, you're having a little insomnia, a few irritable moods—things that are no fun, but may not cross the line? Also, consider whether your symptoms are those that can be effectively treated with HRT, or whether there might there be better ways to address them. If your main symptoms are emotional, for instance, you might ask your doctor about other drugs for depression and anxiety. Also, consider whether you could treat symptoms locally: If you're not having hot flashes, vaginal dryness can be effectively treated with moisturizers and, possibly, an estrogen cream.

❒ List the symptoms that you're most anxious to treat: _____

_____

Step 2. Consider Your Temperament

What are your feelings toward medical treatment and drugs? Some people just don't like the idea of drugs, or have trouble keeping to a regular schedule of medication. Some prefer a milder, more "natural" form of therapy, such as estrogenic foods and herbs. Others, on the other hand, have no confidence in alternative therapies and don't want to spend months experimenting with them when stronger prescription medications are available. Try to stay in your comfort zone in terms of your attitudes.

❏ I'm comfortable with the idea of taking medication.

❏ I'm apprehensive about taking medication or HRT in particular because:

_____

Step 3. Consider Your Personal Risks for Breast Cancer

Do you have any of the following risk factors?

❏ Mother or sister diagnosed with breast cancer

❏ Never having been pregnant

❏ Having a first pregnancy over the age of thirty

❏ A previous breast biopsy or a prior diagnosis of carcinoma in situ (precancer) in your breast

❏ A positive test for the BRCA1 or BRCA2 gene

❏ High alcohol consumption (more than two drinks per day)

❏ Being more than 20 percent over your ideal weight

Step 4. Consider Your Personal Risks for Osteoporosis and Heart Disease

Evaluate your risk using the tables in chapter 7. If you find that you have risk factors for these diseases, ask yourself whether they are factors that you might be able to address by making lifestyle improvements or taking other types of medication. If your main risk factor for heart disease is a high cholesterol level, for instance, the first line of therapy is a class of drugs called statins. (ERT may be taken *in addition to* these drugs, but shouldn't be taken *instead.*) Likewise, consider whether more exercise or dietary modifications, with your doctor's supervision, might be a better place to start.

Step 5. Talk to Your Doctor

Now that you've considered everything that might weigh into your decision, talk it over with your doctor. He or she should be able to help you evaluate the risks and benefits of hormone replacement for your individual case. Ask your doctor to provide information about a safe *range* of choices, so that you can feel empowered to use your self-knowledge and intuition to choose the one that's best for you.

What to Expect at the Doctor's Office

Your first visit to the doctor to discuss possible menopausal symptoms is a very important meeting. To get the most out of it:

• Make a specific, separate appointment for a consultation to discuss menopause and hormone replacement. Don't try to have the discussion at the tail end of a routine physical, because your doctor will not have scheduled enough time to do the discussion justice.

• Come prepared to talk about your symptoms. Try to be as organized as you can. Keeping a journal will help your doctor get a better idea of the patterns of symptoms. Narrow your discussion to the three to five symptoms that are bothering you most.

• Come prepared with a family history.

• Don't worry if your test results don't match your experience. I've heard so many stories of women with terrible symptoms being told by their doctors that, since their test results were normal, they weren't perimenopausal. Your lab values are *not* the whole story—and it's important to find a doctor who agrees. Regardless of your test results, your doctor should consider your symptoms and look for ways to make you feel comfortable and sound again.

• Come prepared with a list of questions to ask. Here are some of the topics you may want to ask your doctor to address:

> • Bioidentical hormones and compounded formulas
> • Scheduling a follow-up appointment to, if necessary, make adjustments to your formula and dosage

- Lifestyle recommendations
- The bone and heart benefits of HRT, and how important they are in your case
- Medications other than HRT that could address your health concerns
- A schedule of checkups (mammogram, pap smear, pelvic exam, bone screening, and so on)
- Other questions: _____

- _____

- _____

A Final Word . . .

Whether you decide to deal with your symptoms through exercise and diet alone, or with HRT, remember this: Menopause is much more than just a set of symptoms. As I've said throughout this book, it's a call to get in touch with what's important to you in life. When you delve into the spiritual issues at midlife, you emerge a different person—powerful and strong, with new interests and priorities. Whatever helps you past your symptoms to focus on those important life issues has played a valuable role.

Resource List and Suggested Reading

Government Agencies

National Cancer Institute, Office of Cancer Communications, Bethesda,
MD 20892; Cancer Information Service, (800)-4-CANCER:
http://www.nci.nih.gov

National Heart, Lung, and Blood Institute, NHLBI Information Center, Box
30105, Bethesda, MD 20824; (301) 592-8573;
http://www.nhlbi.nih.gov

National Institute on Aging, Public Information Office, Building 31, Room
2C234, Bethesda, MD 20892; (301) 496-1752; fax (301) 496-1072;
http://www.nia.nih.gov

National Institutes of Health, Office of Research on Women's Health,
Building 1, Room 201, Bethesda, MD 20892; (301) 402-1770; fax
(301) 827-0926

National Institute of Mental Health, Parklawn Building, Room 17-99,
5600 Fisher Lane, Rockville, MD 20857; (301) 443-3673; fax (301)
443-2578

Organizations

American Heart Association, National Center, 7272 Greenville Avenue, Dallas, TX 75231; (800) 242-8721; http://www.americanheart.org

American Menopause Foundation, Inc., Empire State Building, 350 Fifth Avenue, Suite 822, New York, NY 10118; (212) 714-2398

Boston Women's Health Book Collective, 240A Elm Street, Somerville, MA 02144; (617) 625-0271; http://www.ourbodiesourselves.org

National Osteoporosis Foundation (NOF), 2100 M Street NW, Suite 602, Washington, DC 20036; (202) 223-2226

National Women's Health Network and Clearinghouse, 514 Tenth Street NW, Suite 400, Washington, DC 20004; (202) 628-7814; http://www.womenshealthnetwork.org

North American Menopause Society (NAMS), University Hospital, Department of OB/GYN, 2074 Abington Road, Cleveland, OH 44106; fax (216) 844-3348

WellMax Center for Preventive Medicine, La Quinta Resort and Club, La Quinta, CA 92253; (760) 777-8772

Newsletters and Reports

Harvard Women's Health Watch, P.O. Box 420234, Palm Coast, FL 32142-0234

Health Wisdom for Women, 7811 Montrose Road, Potomac, MD 20854; (310) 424-3700 (monthly newsletter written by Christiane Northrup, an OB/GYN physician well-known for her holistic approach to women's health)

Osteoporosis Report, National Osteoporosis Foundation, 2100 M Street NW, Suite 602, Washington, DC 20037; (202) 223-2226

Books

The Best Alternative Medicine; Dr. Kenneth R. Pelletier; Simon & Schuster, 2000

Bone-Loading: Exercises for Osteoporosis; Ariel Simkin and Judith Ayalon; Prion Publisher, 1996

Clinical Aromatherapy in Nursing; Jane Buckle; Arnold, 1997

Dr. Susan Love's Hormone Book: Making Informed Choices About Menopause; Susan Love with Karen Lindsey; Random House, 1997

For Women Only: A Revolutionary Guide to Overcoming Sexual Dysfunction and Reclaiming Your Sex Life; Jennifer Berman and Laura Berman with Elisabeth Bumiller; Henry Holt, 2001

Full Catastrophe Living: Using the Wisdom of Your Body and Mind to Face Stress, Pain, and Illness; John Kabit-Zinn; Dell Publishing, 1990

Meditation as Medicine; Dharma Singh Khalsa; Pocket Books, 2000

Menopausal Years, The Wise Woman Way: Alternative Approaches for Women 30–90; Susan Weed; Ash Tree Publications, 1992

The Menopause Manager; Joseph L. Mayo and Marry Ann Mayo; Fleming H. Revell, 1998

Menopause: One Woman's Story, Every Woman's Story, A Resource for Making Healthy Choices; National Institute on Aging, NIH Publication No. 01-3886, 2001 (free copies available at 1-800-222-2225)

The Menopause Self-Help Book; Susan M. Lark; Celestial Arts, 1990

Menopause Without Medicine; Linda Ojeda; Hunter House, 1995

Natural Hormone Balance for Women; Uzzi Reiss with Martin Zucker; Pocket Books, 2001

The New Ourselves, Growing Older: Women Aging with Knowledge and Power; Doress, Paula Brown, and Diana Lasking Siegal with the Boston Women's Health Book Collective; Simon & Schuster, 1994

Prescription for Nutritional Healing; James F. Balch and Phyllis A. Balch; Avery Publishing Group, 1997

Recipes for Change: Gourmet Whole Food Cooking for Health and Vitality at Menopause; Lissa DeAngelis and Molly Siple; Dutton, 1996

The Silent Passage: Menopause; Gail Sheehy; Random House, 1992

The Taking Charge of Menopause Workbook; Dosh, Robert and Susan Fukushima, Jane Lewis, Robert Ross, Lynne Steinman; New Harbinger Press, 1997

Taking Hormones and Women's Health: Choices, Risks and Benefits; National Women's Health Network, 2000

What Your Doctor May Not *Tell You About Menopause: The Break-through Book on Natural Progesterone;* John R. Lee and Virginia Hopkins; Warner Books, 1996

What Your Doctor May Not *Tell You About Perimenopause: Balance Your Hormones and Your Life from Thirty to Fifty;* John R. Lee, Jesse Hanley, and Virginia Hopkins; Warner Books, 1999

Women's Bodies, Women's Wisdom; Christiane Northrup; Bantam, Books, 1994

Internet Consumer Information

http://www.consumerlabs.com (great resource for checking quality of nutritional and herbal products)

Progressive Relaxation Script

You can make your own progressive relaxation tape using the following script. Simply read it slowly into a tape recorder, pausing where noted. Speak in a calm, soothing tone; imagine that you're talking to a friend, trying to help her relax. If you want, you can customize the tape in whatever ways you feel might be helpful or more personal.

When you use this tape:

- Sit in a comfortable chair or lie down. Don't listen to this tape while driving!
- Loosen any tight clothing, remove any gum or candy from your mouth, remove glasses or contact lenses (important), take off your shoes, kick back, and relax.
- Turn on low background music, if desired.
- If you're going to use this script to lull yourself to sleep, stop at the end of part 1.

Part I

Close your eyes and let your body begin to relax. Let this be a time for you to unwind and let go of all your daily pressures and responsibilities. Tune in to the background music, and let it move your conscious thoughts into some pleasing and relaxing space. . . . Become aware of your breathing . . . notice how relaxed you feel with each and every breath you exhale . . . Now let this relaxation flow down through your body to your feet . . . feel your feet . . . get in touch with your feet . . . let your feet begin to relax . . . let your feet relax as much as they possibly can . . . and as I move through your body, let each part I mention relax as much as it possibly can . . . Now feel this relaxation flow from your feet gently into your ankles . . . feel your feet and ankles relaxing . . . Now let this relaxation flow from your ankles, up through all the large and small muscles of your legs, into your knees. Such a comfortable, relaxing feeling . . . and with every breath you exhale, let your body continue to relax. Now feel this relaxation flow from your knees into your thighs . . . from your thighs into your hips . . . Now feel this relaxation flow from your hips smoothly into your abdominals . . . and with each breath you exhale, your body continues to relax. Now let this relaxation flow up through all the large and small muscles of your back . . . just let all the tension drain from your back muscles . . . feel your back becoming comfortable and relaxed . . . From your back let this relaxation flow smoothly into your shoulders . . . spreading over your shoulders and down into your chest . . . and with each breath you exhale, let your body continue to relax . . . deeper and deeper relaxed . . . Now feel this relaxation flow from your shoulders down to your elbows . . . from your elbows to your wrists . . . from your wrists into your hands and right out to the ends of your fingertips . . . Now feel this relaxation spreading up into all the large and small muscles of your neck . . . just let all the tension drain from your neck muscles . . . actually feel your neck becoming comfortable and relaxed . . . From your neck feel this relaxation flow up over the back of your head . . . moving across the top of your head and smoothly down into your brow . . . Now let all the muscles around your eyes begin to relax . . . let all the muscles of your eyes begin to relax. Let them relax as much as they possibly can . . . let the muscles of your cheeks relax . . . let the muscles of your chin relax . . . let all your facial muscles completely relax . . . just let all you facial expression drain away . . . let all physical tension drain away . . . let all emotional stress dissipate, and continue drifting down into a deep and comfortable space . . . and while you're drifting . . . let your level of conscious awareness diminish, so you can reach a dreamy, comfortable state where you may drift into a sound and relaxed place.

Now as I count from three down to one . . . I want you to let this relaxation in your body feel deeper . . . three . . . deeper . . . deeper relaxed . . . two . . . deeper and deeper relaxed . . . one . . . very deep and very comfortable and very relaxed . . . from the top of your head down throughout the entire length of your body, all the muscles have relaxed . . . all throughout your body this relaxation grows . . . more and more you grow relaxed . . . You find now that outside noises won't disturb or bother you in any way . . . but instead . . . as you hear the sounds of everyday living, they may actually assist you in relaxing deeper . . . the sound of my voice will also assist you in relaxing . . . and the deeper you relax . . . the more comfortable and peaceful you will become . . . now again I'll count . . . but this time from five down to one . . . and as I count from five down to one . . . I want you to let this relaxation you feel intensify in your body . . . five . . . feel the relaxation beginning to intensify . . . four . . . relaxation intensifying more and more . . . three . . . very comfortable very relaxed . . . two . . . relaxation continuing to deepen . . . one . . . you are becoming more relaxed . . . more comfortable . . . and peaceful . . . from the top of your head to the tips of your toes . . . all the muscles have relaxed and you become more peaceful . . . all tension is draining from your body . . . all anxiety is leaving your mind . . . and with each and every breath you exhale . . . your body keeps right on relaxing . . . deeper and deeper relaxed . . . Now as I count from ten down to one . . . I want you to let your mind relax, just as your body is relaxed . . . and with each count . . . feel your body continuing to relax. Ten . . . your mind is relaxing as your body is relaxed and becoming very peaceful . . . very comfortable . . . very serene . . . nine . . . your mind is relaxing as your body is relaxed . . . and your breathing is becoming regular and slow . . . eight . . . your mind is relaxing as your body is relaxed and you continue drifting down into a deep and comfortable space . . . seven . . . your mind is relaxed as your body is relaxed and your level of conscious awareness is diminishing . . . six . . . just continue to relax . . . five . . . continue to relax . . . four . . . three . . . two . . . one . . . your mind has relaxed, as your body has relaxed and you have become very peaceful . . . very comfortable . . . very serene . . . let your mind fill with pleasant thoughts . . . and your body experience relaxing feelings . . . and continue drifting down into a deep and comfortable space.

Part II

Now I want you to think about the most peaceful place you have ever been . . . and if you can't remember a place, just create one out of your imagination. Make it a beautiful place . . . and see yourself right there . . . feel the presence of this place all around you . . . experience it with as many of your senses as you possibly can . . . perhaps you can smell it . . . hear it . . . see it . . . and even taste it . . . be there as completely as you possibly can . . .

Now . . . I want you to visualize yourself . . . sometime in the future . . . see yourself looking good . . . feeling good . . . working at improving all areas of your life . . . feeling confident about yourself . . . having a good self-image . . . being positive in your attitudes . . . carrying a self-concept of being relaxed and in control . . . having clear thinking . . . good judgment . . . making good decisions . . . Now, as you think about and visualize these things and keep them in your conscious mind during your waking life . . . by degrees, these things will become a part of your everyday feeling . . . and you will become those things you think about.

In a few moments, I will ask you to open your eyes . . . and when you do, I want you to bring back with you this pleasant relaxed feeling in your body . . . feeling refreshed . . . having an alert mind . . . feeling fully awake . . . relaxed and in control . . . and the next time you do this exercise . . . you will be able to go beyond your present state more quickly than you have today . . . and each time you work with yourself . . . you will be able to go deeper, and every suggestion I have given you in the past will reinforce itself . . . Each time you work with yourself, you will be able to reach deep states of concentration where all the suggestions on this tape can be available in your subconscious mind, and become a permanent part of your existence.

Now as I count from one to three, your conscious awareness will increase . . . and on three you will open your eyes feeling refreshed . . . alert . . . fully awake . . . relaxed and in control . . . feeling good about you.

One . . . coming up slowly and comfortably . . . two . . . feeling new life and energy and hope flowing through your body . . . three . . . Open your eyes . . . wide awake . . . fully refreshed . . . relaxed and feeling good about you.

Index

About the Author

Kathy Smith has been a visionary in the fitness industry for more than twenty years. She is among the top sellers of fitness videos, audiotapes, books, and equipment and contributes to *Self* magazine, supporting her mission of educating consumers on being healthy and fit. Smith's more than thirty award-winning videos have sold more than twelve million copies around the world, earning her a place in the Video Hall of Fame. She has been at the forefront of promoting sports and fitness to America's youth and serves on the board of directors of the highly acclaimed University Elementary School at the University of California, Los Angeles. She is also a national ambassador for the March of Dimes. Smith is currently a member of the Woman's Sports Foundation's board of stewards, and she served on the board of trustees from 1993 to 1996. Her company, Kathy Smith Lifestyles, established a scholarship fund through the Woman's Sports Foundation in the name of her two daughters, Kate and Perrie, which demonstrates Smith's ongoing commitment to promoting sports and fitness to young girls. *Kathy Smith's Moving Through Menopause* is Smith's fifth book. Her previous four were *Kathy Smith's Lift Weights to Lose Weight, Kathy Smith's Getting Better All the Time, Kathy Smith's Fitness Makeover,* and *Kathy Smith's WalkFit for a Better Body.*

As a freelance writer and Editorial Director for Health For Life Publications, Robert Miller has written extensively in the areas of health and fitness. He is the coauthor of *Kathy Smith's Lift Weights to Lose Weight.*